THE SQUEEZED MIDDLE

The pressure on ordinary workers in America and Britain

Edited by Sophia Parker

[handwritten notes: x 162 = ney a98m; x 28; 156 N; 215 p 13; 13 p 140]

First published in Great Britain in 2013 by

The Policy Press
University of Bristol
Fourth Floor
Beacon House
Queen's Road
Bristol BS8 1QU
UK
Tel +44 (0)117 331 4054
Fax +44 (0)117 331 4093
e-mail tpp-info@bristol.ac.uk
www.policypress.co.uk

North American office:
The Policy Press
c/o The University of Chicago Press
1427 East 60th Street
Chicago, IL 60637, USA
t: +1 773 702 7700
f: +1 773-702-9756
e:sales@press.uchicago.edu
www.press.uchicago.edu

British Library Cataloguing in Publication Data
A catalogue record for this book is available from the British Library.

Library of Congress Cataloging-in-Publication Data
A catalog record for this book has been requested.

ISBN 978 1 44730 893 5 paperback
ISBN 978 1 44730 894 2 hardcover

Cover design by The Policy Press
Front cover: image kindly supplied by Getty Images
Printed and bound in Great Britain by Hobbs, Southampton
The Policy Press uses environmentally responsible print partners

FSC
www.fsc.org
MIX
Paper from
responsible sources
FSC® C020438

Contents

The squeezed middle

List of tables and figures

Tables

Figures

Notes on contributors

Vidhya Alakeson is the Director of Research and Strategy at the Resolution Foundation, an independent research and policy organisation established to improve the lives of the 11 million people in the UK on low to middle incomes.

Dr Eileen Appelbaum joined the Center for Economic and Policy Research in September 2010 as a senior economist. Previously, she was the Director of the Center for Women and Work at Rutgers University.

Dr Françoise Carré is the Research Director of the Center for Social Policy, McCormack Graduate School, at the University of Massachusetts Boston, and is a member of the global action research policy network Women in Informal Employment: Globalizing and Organizing (WIEGO).

Tamara Draut is Vice President of Policy and Research at Demos, and the author of *Strapped: why America's 20- and 30-somethings can't get ahead* (Doubleday, 2006)

Daniel P. Gitterman is an Associate Professor of Public Policy and a Senior Fellow at the Global Research Institute at the University of North Carolina at Chapel Hill.

Jacob S. Hacker is the Director of the Institution for Social and Policy Studies, and the Stanley B. Resor Professor of Political Science at Yale University. He is also Vice President of the National Academy of Social Insurance, and a former Junior Fellow of the Harvard Society of Fellows.

Professor James Heintz is Research Professor at the Political Economy Research Institute (PERI) at the University of Massachusetts Amherst, and is a member of the global action research policy network Women in Informal Employment: Globalizing and Organizing (WIEGO).

Lane Kenworthy is a Professor in Sociology and Political Science at the University of Arizona, US. He has written extensively on the causes and consequences of living standards, poverty, inequality, mobility, employment, economic growth, social policy, taxes, public opinion and politics in the US and other affluent countries.

Dr Carrie Leana is the George H. Love Professor of Organizations and Management at the University of Pittsburgh, where she is also the Director of the Center for Health and Care Work.

Preeti Mehta is Doorways to Dreams' (D2D's) Director of Project Incubation.

Dr Lawrence Mishel is President of the Economic Policy Institute, a role he assumed in 2002 after joining the Institute as Research Director in 1987.

Sophia Parker was a visiting fellow at the Kennedy School of Government, Harvard University for the duration of this project. Previously, she was the Research and Policy Director of the Resolution Foundation.

Dr James A. Riccio is the Director of Low-Wage Workers and Communities at MDRC. He directed the evaluation of the UK Employment Retention and Advancement programme, and he leads a number of other randomised trials in US, testing innovative employment and anti-poverty programmes.

Dr Heidi Shierholz is an economist at the Economic Policy Institute specialising in labour markets and inequality. She is one of the authors of the Institute's biannual publication *The State of Working America*.

Joanna Smith-Ramani is the Director of Scale Strategies at the Doorways to Dreams (D2D) Fund.

Keith Wardrip joined the Center for Housing Policy as a senior research associate in 2009. Before joining the Center, Keith spent four years as the senior research analyst with the National Low Income Housing Coalition. He earned an MA in Geography at the University of Colorado and a BA in geography at the University of Kentucky.

Foreword

Gavin Kelly and Jared Bernstein

Restoring the link between growth and the living standards of middle- and lower-income families was rightly a focal point of both this and the last US presidential campaign. Now, as the President is sworn into office, the task of seeing through the promise of creating economic security for middle-class America, and reconnecting growth to the fortunes of ordinary working families, must remain at the top of his agenda. Given its centrality to the political economy of both the US and the UK, this issue must define much of politics and policy for the next four years and beyond.

The backdrop is a bleak one, in part because of the depths of the Great Recession. But this doesn't provide anything like a full account. The middle-class families talked about so passionately during the presidential campaign have been going backwards for a generation. For them, the recession was just a deepening of a problem that had been growing for decades. As Larry Mishel and Heidi Shierholz demonstrate starkly in the first chapter of this collection, the early baby boomers born in the decade after the end of the Second World War were the last cohort where the typical family achieved higher living standards than their parents' generation.

A less dramatic but still worrying story has been unfolding in the UK. Typical wages have been flat or falling for nearly a decade. Home ownership has moved out of the reach of a fast-growing swath of the working population, and rents are climbing fast. Less than half of employees are in an employer pension scheme, falling to less than a third in the private sector. A worryingly high proportion of households are already paying such large chunks of their income to meet mortgage costs that they risk going underwater when interest rates eventually return to normal levels. Overall, low- to middle-income Britain finds itself in a highly precarious economic position and forecasts indicate a gloomy decade ahead.

Of course, some things get lost in translation in any comparison with the United States. The US middle class has always had a hazier and more inclusive feel, lacking the social affectations and exclusivity that the term is freighted with in the UK. As a consequence, the UK's political leaders continually strain to find the right language to describe the group whether it be 'hard-working families', 'the squeezed middle' or 'strivers'. Nor have low- and middle-income households in the UK experienced anything like the wage squeeze or house price collapse that has afflicted their American counterparts. And, mercifully, the NHS removes one of the most brutal sources of American insecurity, as well as alleviating the downward pressure on wages that employer-based healthcare generates.

However, there are some basic economic facts of life that are common across the two economies. A move towards full employment is vital for widely shared wage growth, as Lane Kenworthy's essay in this collection emphasises. In addition, we will need strategies to lift low pay, address skills gaps and help workers to progress up the earnings ladder if growth is truly to be shared. How to deliver this, however, is a major problem that public policy in both countries has yet to deal with effectively.

This is the challenge to which this collection responds. It brings together some of the leading thinkers and policy experts in the US to reflect on the problems facing the middle class there, how these relate to the experience in the UK, and how policy could respond in both countries. Jacob Hacker establishes the outlines of this policy agenda in his contribution, emphasising both the too-often-overlooked importance of improving market outcomes rather than relying exclusively on government redistribution and the need for new forms of collective voice and action for the middle class. Other experts fill in the policy detail addressing issues from precarious employment and savings policy to strategies for growing private investment in housing.

Whether it be childcare or training, the minimum wage or tax credits, financial market oversight, job creation or wage bargaining, there is no shortage of ideas seeking to reconnect growth with gain for working people. The need to put these ideas into practice is greater than ever. But given the experience of the last generation in the US, it is clear that shifting policy direction so as to rewire American capitalism to deliver shared growth will require political ambition on the scale of Roosevelt's. As in the Clinton–Blair era, elements of the agenda that emerges in the US will find an echo in the UK. The fate of the US middle class is likely to reveal some of what is in store for the UK.

Gavin Kelly is the Chief Executive of the Resolution Foundation and former Deputy Chief of Staff to the Prime Minister.

Jared Bernstein is Senior Fellow at the Center for Budget and Policy Priorities in Washington DC and former Executive Director of the Vice-President's Middle Class Working Families Task Force.

A note on terminology

The Resolution Foundation focuses on people living on low to middle incomes. This means people living in households below middle (median) income, but above the bottom 10%, and not heavily reliant on means-tested benefits.

In technical terms, the Foundation defines this group as adults living in working-age households in income deciles two to five who receive less than one fifth of their gross household income from means-tested benefits (excluding tax credits). As such, it is an income-based definition, rather than one based on earnings. For the purposes of the income distribution, the Foundation uses 'equivalised' household incomes to take account of the importance of different household sizes and compositions. In some cases, where the data makes it necessary, this definition is simplified.

Defined in this way, 11 million working-age adults live in low- to middle-income households in Britain today, making up one third of the working-age population. Because the Resolution Foundation's definition takes into account household size, the income boundaries of the group depend on the number of children living in a household. For example, couples with no children fall into the group if their incomes (from all sources) range from £12,000 to £30,000 a year, while couples with three children fall into the group if their incomes range from £19,200 to £48,500 a year.[1]

While these households may best be understood as 'low to middle income' in the UK, they are just as likely to be labelled 'middle class' in the US. A US Department of Commerce report for the White House Middle Class Taskforce defines middle class as those families living between the 25th and 75th percentiles. The following table highlights the income levels for families that would fall into this definition.

Income levels for selected families, 2008

	In the distribution of two-parent, two-child families	In the distribution of one-parent, two-child families
25th percentile	$50,800	$13,200
Median	$80,600	$25,200
75th percentile	$122,800	$44,000
Poverty line	$21,800	$17,300

Note: Calculations are based on the income distribution of each family type with two children under the age of 18.

Sources: US Census Bureau, Current Population Survey, 2009 Annual Social and Economic (ASEC) Supplement and Economics and Statistics Administration (ESA) calculations.

For US analysts, middle-class living standards are not determined by income alone. Aspiration and life choices matter as much as having enough money to cover basic expenses, such as health care, car insurance, housing costs and food.[2] There are stark regional variations in the US: whereas the median wage in Boston is US$65,000, it is just US$35,000 in rural Nebraska, and so some analysts define the middle class in relation to a local rather than national median wage. On the basis of these definitions, one in three working American families find that employment does not guarantee a decent living standard, and one in five families find that their wages plus any benefits they receive do not cover their household bills and living costs for the area in which they live.[3]

For the purposes of this volume, each of the contributors is writing about people living in households at or below the median, where the majority of income is derived from wages. Even if the terminology varies between the US and the UK, conceptually, the writers here are talking about the same group – a group that faces unique challenges as a result of their position in the income distribution. People on low to middle incomes are, in many senses, both 'too rich' and 'too poor'. They are too rich to be traditionally considered in need of state support, yet too poor to thrive independently in important private markets, from housing to social care. Members of the group are mostly in work, and so have limited time. They are often on low or modest wages, so also have limited money.

Notes

[1] For more information on the group, and the technical aspects of this definition, see Whittaker, M. (2012) *The essential guide to squeezed Britain*, London: Resolution Foundation, a comprehensive audit of the economic position of people living on low to middle incomes.

[2] See US Department of Commerce (2010) 'Middle class in America: a report prepared for the White House Middle Class Taskforce'. Available at: http://www.commerce.gov/sites/default/files/documents/migrated/Middle%20Class%20Report.pdf

[3] Abelda, R. and Boushey, H. (2007) 'Bridging the gaps: a study of how work supports work in ten states', CEPR (Center for Economic and Policy Research) and CSP (Center for Social Policy). Available at: http://www.bridgingthegaps.org/publications.html

Introduction

Sophia Parker

The American Dream – that if you work hard, you get ahead – is faltering. Over the last generation, the US has experienced the loss of mass upward mobility: it is no longer the case that each generation can expect to do better than the last. A growing gap between productivity and pay, a sharp rise in economic inequality, and limited social mobility have combined to create a squeeze on middle-class living standards whose origins stretch back to well before the most recent recession. This economic malaise is not unique to the US, but it is notably pronounced there.

Historically, the UK has looked different. Our stronger welfare safety net and more generous benefits have helped to ensure that the income instability that is so pronounced in the US is much less significant here. While the UK's employment protection framework is weak compared to other European countries, our inclusive rights-based model gives workers greater security than their US counterparts. Family structure is more stable, with positive effects on household income and economic security. And although the most recent recession is deeper and more prolonged than the downturns of the 1980s and 1990s, unemployment remains lower in the UK than in the US.

But while many commentators continue to emphasise the differences between the US and UK labour markets, there are early warnings signs in the UK that we should heed. Pay is no longer tracking economic growth: median earnings fell for British men between 2003 and 2008, while Gross Domestic Product (GDP) grew by 11%. On the basis of Office of Budget Responsibility projections, wages will be lower in 2015 than they were in 2001. Both countries have witnessed the emergence of a startling gap between the rich and the rest, the like of which has not been seen since early in the 20th century. In 1973, 5.4% of wage and salary income earned in the US went to the top 1% of earners, but by 2007, that had more than doubled to 12.2%.[1] Britain's top 1% of earners received 6.1% of total earnings in 2010, an increase of 71% since 1977.

It is too early to tell whether these signs of stagnating living standards in the UK will deteriorate into the full-blown crisis of the middle class that is now so apparent in the US. But at the very least, the similarities between the two countries in how the income distribution is changing

1

suggest that we should be paying close attention to what has happened in the US over the last generation.

There is now an extensive literature on the role that factors such as technological change, the growth in international trade and the rise in immigration have played in creating the middle-class squeeze. While acknowledging these factors, the message of many of the contributors to this volume is that the change in the relationship between pay and productivity is neither inevitable nor irreversible. They point to the critical role that economic and social policy, as well as economic trends, have played in getting us to this point.

A comparison of the US and the UK on the question of the limitations and possibilities of policy interventions is instructive. Pointing to the US experience, the chapters here warn us of how policy decisions can make things worse, augmenting and extending wider patterns in the economy. Less obvious, but equally pernicious, the contributors to this volume show how the failure of policies to respond effectively to economic changes has left middle-class families exposed and anxious about their futures.

In contrast, many of the social and economic policies of the last decade have played a clear role in *preventing* the UK from travelling further down the US path. From the unprecedented investment in childcare, to the introduction of the National Minimum Wage, to the extension of employee protections to a greater number of workers, our US counterparts look on with envy at the degree to which British governments have been prepared to respond to contemporary economic challenges in recent years.

But despite these successes, the UK experience also hints at the limitations of policy in today's economic and social environment. Progress towards the groundbreaking commitment to eradicate child poverty has been slower than anticipated or hoped for. Social mobility remains low when compared to other European countries, and low-wage, low-skill jobs are both of poor quality and expanding to occupy a greater proportion of the UK labour market.

Together, the US and the UK tell us a story about the possibilities and the limitations of policy when it comes to addressing the middle-class squeeze. On both sides of the Atlantic, many still vociferously argue that the best thing that government can do for living standards is to get out of the way and stimulate growth – at whatever cost, even if that means loosening the labour market yet further. To counter these views, progressives will need to win the case for a smarter approach. This demands a much more sophisticated understanding of *how* and *where* economic and social policies combine to mitigate or reinforce global social trends. But equally important is the need to recognise that what is happening to middle-income households unpicks many of the great economic truths that have shaped decisions over the last generation.

Core themes of this volume

This volume introduces some of the leading US thinkers on living standards. From a variety of perspectives, the writers reflect on what lessons British policymakers might take from the lopsided growth that the US has experienced. The book is organised into three parts. The opening section sets the scene by looking at recent labour market developments. The middle section considers specific policy issues, from creating quality work, to raising incomes, to building greater economic security. Finally, a concluding section looks ahead to future challenges.

The principal message of this volume is clear: the fate of everyday Americans should be understood as a wake-up call for Britain. Few dispute that outsourcing, globalisation and technological change all have a part to play in explaining the increasingly polarised labour markets of the US and the UK. But the public policy choices made by Congress over the last generation have disproportionately benefited the wealthy, while failing to respond to the new pressures faced by households lower down the income distribution.

Building a consensus about how to address the living standards issue is an urgent task. The crisis of everyday voters now needs to be the driving force of UK politics. Parties need to work together to focus aggressively on a long-term economic and industrial strategy that puts decent jobs and broad-based prosperity – rather than growth alone – at its heart.

Against this backdrop, this section outlines three core themes that cut across many of the chapters of this volume.

The sharp edge of the flexible labour market

The flexible labour market has been held up as a successful model for some years now. And yet the writers here repeatedly describe the failures of this model – which are hitting low earners hardest. Of American jobs today, 29% pay below the median wage, and do not provide health or pension benefits. Job tenure has dropped by 20% for male manual workers in the UK, while temping is one of the fastest-growing occupations of the last decade. These kinds of 'lousy jobs' are concentrated in low-paid, low-skill sectors, and are part of an increasingly polarised labour market that leaves many low earners working hard, playing by the rules and yet failing to get ahead.

Unpredictable hours, poor job quality and a lack of fringe benefits matter as much as wages when it comes to understanding living standards – and the data suggest that, by these measures, things are getting worse. A greater proportion of American workers are in precarious employment than their British counterparts. But with low-paid, low-skilled jobs set to rise in both countries over the next 10 years, governments and employers alike will need to do much more to address the issues of job quality and security more effectively.

There are certainly policies that could make a difference in this sphere. Understanding more about what works when it comes to skill ladders and occupational upgrading is an obvious priority. The authors here also argue that the UK should defend and, indeed, extend the employment protections it already has: the US shows how hard workers are hit in their absence. But the fate of low-paid workers in the UK and the US begs a deeper question about the efficacy and fairness of the flexible labour market model that has been pursued by both countries. Four out of five American workers agree that 'no matter what you hear about the economy, working families are falling behind'.[2] The consequences of this collective loss of hope are likely to reverberate across society and through generations. The evidence presented here forces an uncomfortable question: do the shortcomings of the flexible labour model now outweigh the benefits for the majority of workers?

The importance of boosting pay checks and redistribution

Resolution Foundation analysis shows that transfers between households via the tax and benefit system are doing more heavy lifting today than ever before. In 1977, they topped up the incomes of low-earning households by 1%. This has now quadrupled to nearly 4%. US commentators point to the crucial role that such redistributive policies have played in the UK to counteract the growth in market inequalities in recent years. Coupled with tax policies that disproportionately benefit the rich, the limited nature of such redistributive programmes in the US certainly explains some of the differences between the two countries when it comes to rising inequality.

But while few dispute the ongoing importance of transfers between households, many of the contributors here underline the importance of the government's role in shaping market wages as well as post-tax household incomes. Not so long ago, UK and US governments played a far more interventionist role in this sphere. However, much of this architecture has been eroded or destroyed over the last generation. For example, the US minimum wage, never indexed, was worth less in real terms in 2010 than it was in 1955. Deregulation of labour markets and a steep decline in unionisation on both sides of the Atlantic have all but decimated the bargaining power of low earners when it comes to wages.

At the same time, the 'financialisation' of the economy means that firms today face greater competition and heavy pressure from shareholders to maximise short-term profits at the expense of labour and wages.[3] Complex supply chains and outsourcing practices put greater distance between employers and employees, resulting in diffuse wage-setting processes that undermine wage norms and reduce employer accountability for working standards.[4] The net effect of these shifts has been to reduce workers' power and diminish their wages.

The question of how to raise wages in this new world is addressed by a number of the contributors to this volume. The UK will need to fight to maintain the National Minimum Wage at a decent level. This, along with the protection of existing family-friendly rights, is a basic minimum. But we will also need to build on emerging initiatives and ideas. From the LAANE in Los Angeles to Citizens UK in London,[5] living wage campaigns on both sides of the Atlantic are pioneering a new approach that simultaneously relies on government support and changes in employer practices. 'Shared capitalism' models, advocated by Richard Freeman and others, link employee compensation to company performance and broad-based stock options, which give workers the same access to capital earnings that their high-paid bosses have.[6] As well as focusing on government action, there will need to be a wider sea-change in norms about wage inequalities and the responsibility that organisations have to their workers.[7]

The need to address new pressures in family life

The declining value of male wages has been hidden by one of the most significant transformations of the 20th century: the mass entry of women into the labour market. While men's hours stayed unchanged, working wives in middle-income American families increased their labour by almost 500 hours between 1979 and 2006 – the equivalent of three extra months of full-time work.[8] Women's extra hours accounted for 75% of the growth in household income for the middle 20% of families between 1979 and 2004 – a phenomenon that has been mirrored in the UK.

Thanks to the stagnation of male wages, women's earnings are no longer a luxury but an essential part of the budget for many households. Tony Blair's adage that 'work is the best route out of poverty' is too simplistic: 'living in a two-earner household is the best route out of poverty' is a better reflection of the evidence, albeit less of a catchy phrase.[9] Closing the gender pay gap, providing decent childcare and requiring more flexible working practices are not only about social policy or women's rights, they are also central to the future economic security of middle-class households.

The contributors here universally acknowledge that the UK has done a much better job than the US in addressing the new pressures of family life. Public spending on family benefits in Britain stood at 3.6% of GDP in 2007, compared to an Organisation for Economic Co-operation and Development (OECD) average of 2.2%, and a US investment just 1.2% of GDP. Investments in childcare over the last decade have been sustained and significant. For now at least, family-friendly policies, such as maternity leave and the right to request flexible working, are established.

Nevertheless, Resolution Foundation analysis shows that a family with two young children will need to earn an additional £3,700 a year to compensate for the cut in eligible childcare support from 80% to 70%.[10] Within the last year alone (between July 2010 and July 2011), an additional 32,000 women chose to look after their children rather than seek work.[11] There are concerns that the introduction of the Universal Credit from 2013 will worsen this situation further. There is little room for complacency despite our stronger foundations in family-friendly policies when compared to the US. Historically, social policy has been developed around an assumed male breadwinner/female carer model, which resulted in the underdevelopment of care. Today, protecting existing family-friendly rights, and extending social policies designed to support families juggling paid work and caring responsibilities, will be a vital part of improving the living standards of low and middle earners.

Introducing the contributions to the volume

This section briefly introduces the following chapters and provides a summary of the remainder of this volume. The authors here include economists, political scientists and policy analysts. This diversity underlines the fact that to address declining living standards, action is needed on many fronts: economic and social policy, political leadership, organisational practices, and cultural norms.

Section 1 – Setting the scene: a rising tide no longer lifts all boats

The first section of this volume looks at trends in wages and jobs in the US since the 1970s. The post-war period in the US was characterised by a narrowing of the income gap (which had reached historically high levels in the 1920s[12]) and a booming economy. Comparatively little international competition, strong unions and a New Deal consensus about the importance of fairness meant that firms were passing on the fruits of growth to their workers. Since the 1970s, economic growth has continued. But, as Heidi Shierholz and Lawrence Mishel show in Chapter 1.1, disaggregating this data tells a different story: the incomes of the poorest fifth increased by just 16% while the incomes of the richest fifth soared by 95%.[13] Mishel and Shierholz show that there are also concerning developments for households in the middle of America's income distribution. From the 1970s onwards, median family incomes have not kept up with economic growth. While the incomes of higher-income families have grown rapidly, less well-off households have experienced slow, no or negative growth. Even if 2000, rather than the late 1970s, is taken as the starting point, the picture looks bleak – in Shierholz and Mishel's words, it was 'America's lost decade'.

Lane Kenworthy in Chapter 1.2 reinforces this analysis, showing that there has only been one brief period since the 1970s in which real wages in the bottom half of the American income distribution have increased – the late 1990s. During this unusual period, unemployment was low but this did not trigger rises in inflation. Instead, the downward trajectory of wages for low earners was momentarily reversed, and the benefits to workers of a high employment rate appeared to far outweigh the risks of price pressures. Given this evidence, Kenworthy argues that while it might not be a panacea, a high employment rate is an important policy goal when it comes to addressing stagnant wage growth, steeper rates of inequality and stubbornly high poverty levels. The challenge is to achieve that goal without raising inequality.

Section 2 – Policy lessons

The contributors in Section 1 consider the large-scale economic trends shaping the decline in living standards for families in the US and the UK. In Section 2, the contributors shift their focus to explore more specific policy areas to address the crisis in middle-class living standards. There are many ways in which this can be done, as these chapters show – and, in reality, an effective approach to raising incomes is likely to require action on all the elements described here.

Creating quality work: supporting low earners in the modern labour market

Both the UK and the US have become service economies over the last 30 years. Over this period, the new jobs that have been added to the economy are very different to the typical jobs of older generations. As the economy has become increasingly service-driven, manufacturing jobs – with relatively high wages, good job security and substantial fringe benefits – are being replaced by jobs that are part time, low wage and come with few, if any, benefits. Eileen Appelbaum and Carrie Leana explore these issues through focusing on the caring occupations, given that care is a key sector where low earners work. Considering the projected growth in these jobs, they argue that governments will need a clearer strategy to improve pay, job quality and opportunities for progression in the care sector and other industries that are equally low paid. As well as government action, their chapter points to the importance of shifting employer practices and organisational norms.

The second chapter in this section looks at the extent to which modern jobs induce or protect against economic vulnerability. Drawing on their extensive research in this field, Françoise Carré and James Heintz highlight how 'non-standard' jobs – such as temp workers, agency staff, day labourers and so on – are likely to be more precarious than standard jobs. Non-standard work may not dominate the British labour market but, as Carré and Heintz show, the risks entailed by these jobs are significant. Their chapter underlines the crucial importance of Britain's decision to extend many employment rights to non-standard workers. Without this framework, many more workers would be exposed to economic vulnerabilities, as they are in the US.

Raising incomes: combining redistribution with pre-distribution

The two chapters in this section look beyond increasing hours to consider what can be done to improve hourly wages. They also consider how transfers – particularly tax credits – can be designed to increase incomes for low-earning families.

Jim Riccio's chapter shares the latest evidence from a pioneering study into what works when it comes to supporting career progression for low earners. The results he presents are from the Employment Retention Allowance pilots, trialled in the UK between 2003 and 2006, and developed on the basis of earlier US experiments. Riccio shows the scale of the challenge associated with a skills-led approach to increasing wages. Training *can* make a difference – but only if courses have a clear market value, and only if the new skills developed enable workers to access real job opportunities in their local areas.

The emphasis on work and career progression as a route to economic well-being is important, but it remains the case that the ladder has got longer and the rungs have got further apart. In this context, the redistribution of incomes between households will continue to play a significant part in boosting pay packets.

In the second chapter of this section, Daniel P. Gitterman asks what lessons can be learnt from the US about the different ways in which governments use tax systems to reduce income inequality and boost the incomes of middle-class households. And he asks how sustainable such strategies will be given the projected growth in low-paid jobs on both sides of the Atlantic and the ongoing impact of the recession on unemployment, underemployment and fiscal constraints. Drawing on the evidence, he argues that tax credits and wage policies such as the National Minimum Wage are mutually reinforcing, and equally critical in boosting the pay packets of low and middle earners.

Strengthening economic security: 'the path to mobility is paved with assets'[14]

Financial capital, along with family structure and educational attainment, are the three strongest predictors of economic mobility in the US. A family's ability to build up such assets is crucial to their chances of economic security. Assets can be converted into safety nets and into springboards such as a new home, a college education or savings for retirement. As the saying goes, income is what people use to get by, but assets are what they use to get ahead.

Joanna Smith Ramani and Preeti Mehta show how market failures, poor public policies and individual behaviours have always made it challenging for low-income households to save. Smith Ramani and Mehta highlight the lessons from a number of US experiments in this field. From child savings accounts, to matching schemes, to prize-linked savings, to programmes connecting tax credits with savings goals, this is an area rich in innovation in the US. They argue that more work is needed to evaluate these experiments, and to take them to scale. But beyond this, Smith Ramani and Mehta point to the gross unfairness of government support for asset building in the US that favours the well off. This is a stark reminder to British policymakers that the use of tax incentives to 'nudge' certain behaviours can be deeply distorting as they disproportionately benefit the wealthy.

Housing is a particularly important part of the asset agenda. Home ownership is still a major aspiration, perceived to be a marker of success and a buffer against economic insecurity. Even after the recent crash, 81% of Americans believe that buying a home is the best long-term investment one can make – a figure that has barely changed since 1991. Similarly in the UK, home ownership remains the number one aspiration for the UK's young people. And yet today's generation of young people are finding themselves priced out of the market. Keith Wardrip's contribution describes the growing significance of the private rental sector in the US. This is a trend mirrored in the UK, and affordability and quality are now central issues for the sector on both sides of the Atlantic. Wardrip's chapter explores the mechanisms used by the Federal and local governments in the US to draw private investment into the development of the rented sector.

Section 3 – Looking ahead: a cautionary tale

The final section of this volume explores the interconnections between economic and social inequalities, politics and governance, and public policies. The stagnation of the living standards of middle-class Americans is undoubtedly an economic crisis. But the contributions here show how this economic crisis has also become a political crisis. The clear message from Tamara Draut's and Jacob Hacker's contributions in this section is that Britain must recognise the early warning signs of a similar middle-class squeeze and act swiftly to avoid treading the same path as their transatlantic neighbours. As Diane Coyle has argued, political frictions caused by fiscal pressures will overlay the fractures caused by growing inequalities of income and wealth.[15]

Addressing stagnating living standards must become the driving force of economic and social policy in the UK. For Draut, this means crafting a response to the recession that focuses on more than growth alone. Drawing on a blueprint developed by US think tank Demos, the Economic Policy Institute and The Century Foundation, she calls for a return to the broad-based prosperity of the post-war years.

Jacob Hacker argues that it is not economics alone that has caused the middle-income squeeze, but also economic policy. A positive example of this can be seen in the way that the UK's more generous regime of tax credits and benefits helped to stem the sharp rises in inequality of the 1980s during the 1990s and early 2000s. More worryingly, in the US, the ongoing Bush tax cuts deprive the Federal government of trillions of dollars each year, at the same time that deep cuts are being made to vital public services. Echoing Lane Kenworthy's contribution, Hacker's chapter underlines the importance of assessing the extent to which economic and social policies augment or reduce the growth in market inequalities. Hacker shows that many of the organisations that once represented middle-class households on economic issues – particularly unions – have declined, leaving many people without a voice in the political process. Hacker asks what it would take to reorganise low earners in the absence of unions. It seems that this question is yet to be adequately answered in either the UK or the US.

A wake-up call for the UK

The conclusion to this volume draws attention to the differences between the UK and the US in some important ways. First, economic policy does not disproportionately benefit the rich in the UK to the same extent that it does in the US. Second, our political systems are very different. As the summer of 2011 has shown, the United States' biggest problem is that its system of checks and balances can effectively stymie any action at all. In contrast, power is concentrated heavily in the hands of the Executive in the UK, at the expense of Parliament and local government. Thus, the interplay between the economics of the squeezed middle and politics may look rather different on British soil. Third, the recession has heightened these differences, leaving unprecedented numbers of Americans out of work – and challenging the country's perception that they are a high-inequality but high-employment nation. In contrast, while the drops in employment in the UK have been dramatic, they have not plummeted to the extent some analysts expected given the severity and length of the downturn.

All of these differences indicate that it is not inevitable that the UK is on the same path as the US, despite sharing similar trends in terms of rising inequality and declining living standards. But the contributions here serve as a cautionary tale at a time when many of the things that make the UK different – its stronger welfare state and fuller framework of employment protections, to name just two – are under review. Time and again, the contributors here show how these mechanisms have served to protect British workers from the income instability and insecurity that make the US stand out so uncomfortably among rich nations.

The crisis of middle-class living standards in the US should be a wake-up call to the UK policymaking community. There are already warning signs that low- and modest-income households in the UK are falling behind. Understanding these signs and taking action accordingly should be the single-minded goal of progressive politics today.

Notes

[1] Data from Pikkety, T. and Saez, E. (2010) 'Income inequality in the United States', Table B2. Available at: http://elsa.berkeley.edu/~saez/TabFig2008.xls

[2] Quoted in Newman, K. (2008) *Laid off, laid low: the political and economic consequences of employment insecurity*, New York: Columbia University Press.

[3] Levy, F. and Kochan, T. (2011) 'Addressing the problem of stagnant wages', Employment Policy Research Network. Available at: http://www.employmentpolicy.org/topic/12/research/addressing-problem-stagnant-wages

[4] Weil, D. (2010) 'Fissured employment', working paper, Boston University.

[5] For more information, see: http://www.laane.org/ and http://www.citizensuk.org/

[6] Kruse, D., Freeman, R. and Blasi, J. (eds) (2010) 'Shared capitalism at work: employee ownership, profit and gain sharing, and broad-based stock options (NBER)'. Available at: http://www.nber.org/books/krus08-1/

[7] Hutton, W. (2010) *Them and us: changing Britain and why we need a fair society*, London: Little, Brown and Company.

[8] Middle Class Task Force (2010) 'Annual report of the White House Middle Class Task Force'. Available at: http://www.whitehouse.gov/sites/default/files/microsites/100226-annual-report-middle-class.pdf

[9] Between 2007 and 2010, the risk of poverty was 5% for adults and children in full-working households. It varied from 25% to 35% for part-working families – those where either one adult works and one does not or the only paid work carried out is part time. See Parekh, A., MacInnes, T. and Kenway, P. (2010) *Monitoring poverty and social exclusion 2010*, York: Joseph Rowntree Foundation.

[10] Kelly, G. (2011) 'The Coalition's woes with women', *The New Statesman*. Available at: http://www.newstatesman.com/blogs/gavin-kelly/2011/09/women-support-coalition

[11] Aviva (2011) 'The Aviva family finances report'. Available at: http://www.aviva.com/data/media-uploads/news/File/pdf/2011/family_finances_report_3_aug2011.pdf

[12] Picketty, T. and Saez, E. (2003) 'Income inequality in the United States, 1913–1998', *Quarterly Journal of Economics*, vol 118, pp 1-39. Updated 2007 version available at: http://emlab.berkeley.edu/users/saez

—

[13] Sherman, A. and Stone, C. (2010) 'Income gaps between very rich and everyone else more than tripled in last three decades', Center on Budget and Policy Priorities, June. Available at: http://www.cbpp.org/cms/index.cfm?fa=view&id=3220

[14] Cramer, R., Lopez-Fernandini, A., Guge, L., King, J. and Zimmerman, J. (2010) 'The assets agenda 2011: policy options to promote savings and asset development', New America Foundation. Available at: http://www.newamerica.net/publications/policy/the_assets_agenda_2011

[15] Coyle, D. (2011) *The economics of enough: how to run the economy as if the future matters,* Princeton, NJ: Princeton University Press.

Section I

Setting the scene:
a rising tide no longer lifts all boats

A lost decade, not a burst bubble: the declining living standards of middle-class households in the US and Britain

Larry Mishel and Heidi Shierholz

Before the bursting of the housing bubble and the catastrophic unemployment and underemployment that followed, the fact that the wages and incomes of most American workers were not keeping up with economy-wide productivity growth was one of the most glaring failures of the American economic model. This decoupling of pay and productivity has been the source of much debate in the US. But it is not a uniquely American phenomenon. From Canada to Australia, and, more recently, Germany and the UK, there is now evidence that similar patterns are beginning to emerge in other developed economies around the world.

This chapter indicates that the similarities between the American and British economic models may now be more significant than the differences. US politicians still talk of the 'socialist' healthcare system in the UK as an alien concept, and Brits may look across the Atlantic in horror at our threadbare welfare system, but at a more fundamental level, our countries share a problem. That problem is that a rising tide no longer guarantees that all boats are lifted. In other words, while our nations have got richer, our low- and middle-income households have suffered a stagnation and even decline in their living standards.

In that light, this chapter outlines the major trends in the US in the hope that we can offer some lessons to learn from the unbalanced growth that the US has had over the last generation. These lessons are important for any country hoping to create a more equitable future. Most importantly, we argue that the economic situation we observe today is not simply the product of globalisation and technology. Rather, it is also the result of choices made about economic and social policies. In other words, it is within the gift of politicians and others to usher in a broader-based prosperity in the future – if they want to.

The long-term stagnation of median household income

Figure 1.1.1 tells the basic American story by showing family income growth at the 20th percentile, the median and the 95th percentile, indexed to 100 in 1979 for easy comparison of growth rates at each of these points in the distribution. Between 1947 and the business cycle peak in 1979, income growth was fairly similar across the income distribution – over this period, real family income at the 20th percentile grew 104.1%, at the median it grew by 111.8% and at the 95th percentile it grew by 106.1%. From 1979, however, the lower points of the distribution flattened substantially. Between 1979 and 2009, family income at the 20th percentile *decreased* by 0.8%, family income at the median increased by 11.4% and income at the 95th percentile increased by 43.1%.

In the UK, the story was similar. As Figure 1.1.2 shows, from 1961 to 1979, growth across the income distribution was fairly equal – over this period, real household income at the 30th percentile grew 27.8%, at the median it grew by 31.7% and at the 95th percentile it grew by 30.0%. From 1979, however, the lower points of the distribution flattened substantially, though not as much as they did in the US. Between 1979 and 2009, UK household income at the 20th percentile increased

Figure 1.1.1: Real income growth across the income distribution in the US, 1947–2009

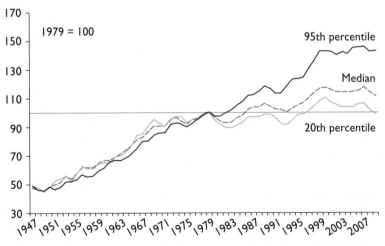

Source: Economic Policy Institute (EPI) analysis of US Census Bureau data, 'Historical income tables', Tables F2 and F5

Divufuer Suci
1979

A lost decade, not a burst bubble

Figure 1.1.2: Real income growth across the income distribution in the UK, 1961–2009

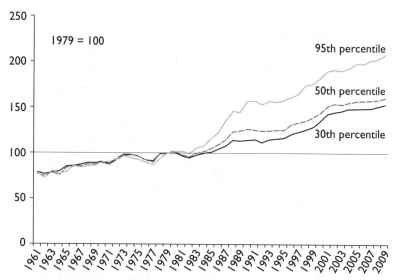

Source: EPI analysis of Institute for Fiscal Studies, 'Inequality and poverty spreadsheet', http://www.ifs.org.uk/fiscalFacts/povertyStats

by 53.1%, household income at the median increased by 60.1%, and income at the 95th percentile increased by 107.7%.

To ground the US case in a historical context in another way, Figure 1.1.3 shows median family income in the US over the life-cycle of the householder, *by birth cohort*. A hint for reading this plot is to start from the bottom right with the earliest cohort, and read counter-clockwise. We follow 10-year birth cohorts, starting with those born 1885–94 and ending nearly 100 years later, with those born 1975–84. The data are only available from 1949 to 2009, so for early cohorts, we do not have the early years of the life-cycle and for more recent cohorts (who are still in the middle of their work-life), we of course do not have the later years of the life-cycle.

This plot tells a crucial story about income growth in the US. First, it shows (unsurprisingly) that as in the UK, family incomes typically increase over the life-cycle of the householder until near retirement age. It also shows that from our first birth cohort up through the early baby boomers (those born 1945–54), the age-income profiles were shifting higher – that is, each cohort saw substantial gains in living standards compared to the cohort that preceded them – though the gains from cohort to cohort slowed over that time. But perhaps most importantly, it shows that after the early baby boomers, the progress

Figure 1.1.3: Median family income in the US over the life-cycle, by birth cohort

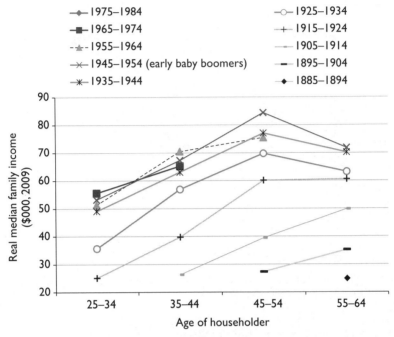

Source: EPI analysis of US Census Bureau data, 'Historical income tables', Table F11

completely stops – birth cohorts following the early baby boomers have seen no additional improvements. *In other words, the early baby boomers were the last cohort where the typical family saw higher living standards than the cohort that preceded them.*

Such a shocking loss of mass upward mobility strikes at the heart of the American Dream. We cannot yet see such patterns in the UK, but this does not mean that there is no cause for concern, given that these trends followed the stagnation in median American wages. The decoupling of median pay and productivity in the UK is a relatively recent phenomenon and policymakers should be paying close attention to how it impacts upon the living standards of successive generations.

What lies behind this story?

While our concern is low- to middle-income households, it is important to look at what is happening elsewhere in the income distribution too. In the business cycle peak of 1973, 9.2% of the total income earned in the US went to the top 1% of households, but by the business cycle peak of 2007, that had more than doubled to 23.5%.[1] In the UK, during the 1970s, the bottom 50% of earners enjoyed a greater share of wages than the top 10%. By 1990, this situation had reversed, and the gap between the two groups subsequently stretched. By 2010, the top 10% took more wages home than the bottom 50%. This pattern is even more pronounced if annual, rather than weekly, wages are taken account of, reflecting the growing significance of bonuses in an economy where the financial sector has boomed in recent years.

In both countries, some of these increases are due to the fact that a much larger portion of national income accrued to capital (i.e. interest, dividends and realised capital gains), and capital income became more concentrated at the top. In 2007, income from interest, dividends and rent represented 18.4% of all market-based personal income in the US, much higher than the 13.9% and 15.1% shares in, respectively, 1973 and 1979.[2] Similarly, in the UK, the capital share of income grew by 6% between 1977 and 2010. In percentage terms, this increase may seem insignificant, but the magnitude of the figures involved tells a different story: a three percentage point rise equates to £29 billion in 2010 prices, a third of the UK government's spending on education.[3]

As more income went to capital over the last few decades, there was also an increased concentration of such income at the top. According to data from the Congressional Budget Office, the top 1% of Americans received 34.2% of all capital income in 1979, but their share rose to 58.6% in 2000 and to 65.3% in 2005 (the latest data available). Thus, the top 1% doubled its share of capital income during a period where capital income became more plentiful.[4]

But while more income went to capital, this is not the primary explanation behind the stagnation in the household incomes of ordinary workers over the last generation. For this, we need to turn to inequalities in wage and salary income, which have risen dramatically in the US and the UK. In 1973, 5.4% of wage and salary income earned in the US went to the top 1% of earners, but by 2007, that had more than doubled to 12.2%.[5] While the UK's top 1% of earners may only receive 6.1% of total earnings in 2010, this is still an increase of 71% since 1977.

Whereas Figure 1.1.1 looked at *total household incomes*, Figure 1.1.4 considers the growing gap between *hourly pay* and productivity (the value of goods and services produced per hour worked on average). From the post-Second World War period into the 1970s in the US, productivity and pay grew in tandem, as economic theory would predict. But starting in the mid-1970s, productivity began to far outpace the growth of compensation. Between 1973 and 2009, productivity in the US grew by 92.6% while the average hourly wage for production

Figure 1.1.4: US wages and compensation stagnate

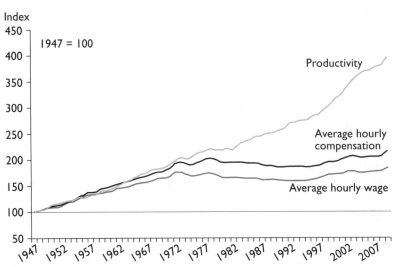

Source: EPI analysis of US Bureau of Economic Analysis and US Bureau of Labor Statistics data

and non-supervisory workers grew by 4.3% and their average hourly compensation (wages plus benefits) grew by just 10.3%. Furthermore, virtually all of that wage growth came in the boom period of the late 1990s when employment was high, as Lane Kenworthy discusses in Chapter 1.2.

Looking only at the period from 1973 on, Figure 1.1.5 shows the vastly unequal wage growth across the US wage distribution. Between 1973 and 2007, when productivity grew by 84.0%, and the 95th percentile grew by 33.1%, the median wage grew by just 6.2% and the 20th percentile wage grew by just 5.2%. The break in the tight relationship between productivity growth and wage growth for most workers meant that the gains of the last three and a half decades went almost entirely to the upper echelons of the wage distribution.

Importantly, the wage growth rates in Figure 1.1.5 mask significant gender differences over this period. Figure 1.1.6 shows median annual earnings for full-time, full-year workers from 1973 to 2010 by gender. Between 1973 and 2010, male earnings have changed little, actually slightly decreasing from $49,065 in 1973 to $47,715 in 2010. In other words, *wages for the median man working full time, full year have seen no growth in almost four decades.* The trend over time for women is very different, largely because of structural factors related to broader social changes, including women becoming more attached to the labour force, increasing their educational attainment and entering higher-paying

Figure 1.1.5: Wages at the high end in the US are growing faster

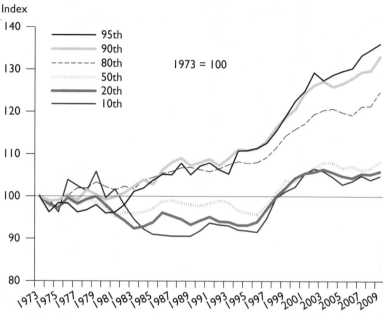

Source: EPI analysis of US Census Bureau, 'Current population survey, outgoing rotations group'

occupations. Particularly in the 1980s and 1990s, women saw substantial earnings growth. However, though the median female worker saw larger wage gains than the median male worker over this period, both dramatically failed to keep pace with productivity growth. And furthermore, with the weakness in the labour market over the 2000s, women's earnings have largely levelled off. Women's earnings have grown less than 1% since 2002, when the recovery from the early 2000s' recession began, after having grown almost 30% from 1979 to 2002.

Again, the similarities are far more striking than the differences when the UK picture is compared to the American trends presented here. Figure 1.1.7 shows that between 2002/03 and 2008/09, the average household in the low- to middle-income group in the UK saw its income rise by £143. This small increase was made up of a loss over the period of £610 of income from male employment, which was offset by an increase of £301 from female employment and a huge boost from tax credits.[6] It is too early to point to a fundamental shift in the relationship between wages and productivity, but, nevertheless, the early stages of the American trend are in evidence.

It is often assumed that the rising 'college wage premium' (the gap between the wages of college graduates and high school graduates)

Figure 1.1.6: Earnings for full-time, full-year workers by gender from 1973 to 2010

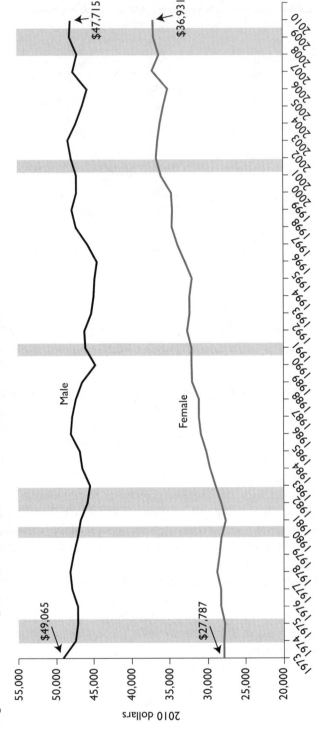

Note: Shaded areas denote recession.

Source: EPI analysis of US Census Bureau, 'Current population survey, 1967–2011 annual social and economic supplements', Table P-41, 'Work experience – All workers by median earnings and sex: 1987–2010'

Figure 1.1.7: Change in annual net equivalent household income, low- to middle-income households, 2002/03 to 2008/09

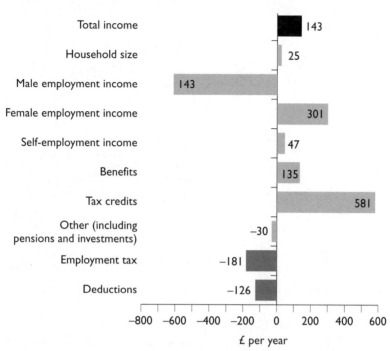

Source: Institute for Fiscal Studies analysis for the Resolution Foundation: Brewer, M. and Wren Lewis, L. (2012) *Why did Britain's households get richer? Decomposing UK household income growth between 1968 and 2008-09*, London: Resolution Foundation

largely accounts for the growth of overall wage inequality in the US. We will not attempt to thoroughly break down the rise of wage inequality into its various components here, but we will offer a few findings showing that rising wage inequality is about much more than increases in the college premium.

It is true that the college wage premium has increased in the US: in 1979, college-educated workers made around 23% more than workers with only a high school degree, and by 2007, that had doubled to around 46%. But, importantly, in 2007, 31% of workers had a college degree or more (21% had a college degree only, and 10% had an advanced degree), while most of the income gains over this period have gone to a much smaller slice. The pay of college graduates is almost as disconnected from productivity growth as the pay of high school graduates. Figure 1.1.8 shows the gap between the growth of productivity and that of the hourly compensation of both the median worker with a college degree (and no additional degree) and the

Figure 1.1.8: Productivity and median wage by education in the US, 1995–2007

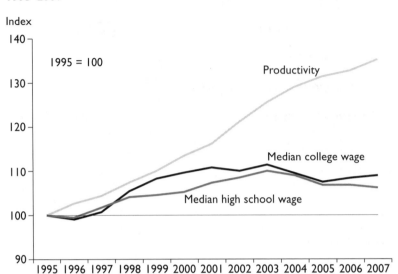

Source: EPI analysis of US Bureau of Labor Statistics and US Bureau of Economic Analysis

median worker with a high school degree (and no additional degree) since 1995 in the US. Hourly compensation grew in the late 1990s for both groups of workers, though still lagged productivity growth. After the momentum of the wage growth in the 1990s faded, there was *no* growth in pay, though productivity continued to climb. In other words, a college degree offered far from a guarantee that wage growth would outpace economy-wide productivity growth.

More of the rise in wage inequality can be explained by increased wage gaps among workers *within* the same education group (eg rising wage inequality *among* workers with a college degree) than by wage gaps between workers of different education levels (eg college wages rising relative to high school wages).[7] One reason behind the rising inequality among those with a college degree may be the rise of finance; the share of the economy accounted for by salaries and profits in the financial sector has multiplied and a large share of those individuals who have seen their incomes soar in the past three decades work in this sector.[8] On the other hand, many college graduates are now working in jobs that do not require a college degree.

The evidence on rising within-group inequality bears out in the UK experience too. In an exhaustive study, Gosling et al conclude that this 'college premium' accounts for no more than a third of the dispersion in male wages between the 1970s and the 1990s.[9] But within those with a graduate education, analysis by Holmes and Mayhew identifies a two-tiered labour market in the UK, with the graduate premium remaining approximately constant across most of the wage distribution with the exception of the top 20%, where it has risen very fast.[10]

Looking ahead

Employment projections in the US and the UK alike indicate that there will be continued 'occupational upgrading' in the years to come – in other words, there will be more jobs in the future requiring higher qualifications and training, and offering slightly better wages. In the UK, *managers and senior officials* are projected to grow by 1.7% per annum between 2007 and 2017, *professional occupations* by 1.5% and *associate professional and technical occupations* by 1.4%.[11]

Turning to the US, Table 1.1.1 presents the results of a shift-share analysis of the 754 occupations for which the Bureau of Labor Statistics provides projections from 2006 to 2016. Given the characteristics of jobs in 2006, this analysis shows what job characteristics will be in 2016 if the projections are realised. The table shows that employment will shift to occupations with higher median annual wages, but the effect will be to raise annual wages by about 0.1% per year, not a large change. It also shows that the jobs of the future will require greater education credentials, but not to any great extent. In 2006, the occupational composition of jobs required that 27.7% of the workforce have a college degree or more. According to US Bureau of Labor Statistics projections, this share will rise by one percentage point to 28.7% by 2016. The demand for workers with a high school degree or less will fall slightly, from 43.6% to 42.6% over the 2006–16 period.

The projections in Table 1.1.1 show that occupational upgrading will continue in the future, as the jobs created will be in occupations with

Table 1.1.1: Effect of changing occupational composition on education and training requirements and earnings, 2006–16

Job characteristic	2006	2016	Change 2006–16
Annual earnings ($2004)	38,087	38,520	1.1%
Education level			
High school or less	43.5	42.6	–0.9
Some college	28.7	28.7	0.0
College or more	27.7	28.7	1.0
	100.0	100.0	

Source: EPI analysis of US BLS projections for 754 occupations and their skill and education levels.

somewhat higher wages and educational and training requirements. This trend has been evident over the last century, and the developments in the future do not appear to be extraordinary in any sense. In other words, our key challenge is not generating a greatly expanded supply of college graduates. Rather, a key question is access, particularly for the many working–class and minority children who are now in large part excluded from the acquisition of college degrees in the US. In the UK, too, there is a risk that the pace at which workers are becoming increasingly well-qualified will leave many of these skills underutilised. Many apparently good jobs continue to earn middle wages despite higher-status job titles. For example, in financial intermediation, a sector that has performed relatively well over the last two decades, there has clearly been a growth in high–wage managerial jobs: those earning over £1,500 per week increased from around 5% in 1993 and 2000, to 10% in 2008. However, between 2000 and 2008, there was also a growth in the proportion of managers in this sector earning less than £400 per week (from 24% to 30%).[12]

Ultimately, we must provide a much broader path to prosperity that encompasses future workers at every education level. As Josh Bivens argues in his book *Failure by design*,[13] and as Jacob Hacker argues in Chapter 3.2, it is not the economy that has limited strong income growth for most families, but rather the *economic policies* pursued and the distribution of economic and political power that are the limiting factors. This is good news for the UK and other countries that are beginning to exhibit the 'great decoupling' of pay and productivity that defines the contemporary US economy: it means that there are choices that can be made. But it is also a warning – broad-based prosperity will not happen via the market alone.

So what could this mean in policy terms? The key point is that such a major rewriting of the economic relationship between growth and gain is unlikely to be solved by a single 'silver bullet'. Key elements of a programme for shared prosperity would involve a stronger worker voice and union organising,[14] financial sector regulation to dampen the monopoly power of financial firms and reduce the labour market rents paid to its employees, raising the real value of the minimum wage so that it has the power to lift the bottom end of the income distribution, and managing global integration more carefully so that workers (and not just capital-owners) are protected from unfair competition.

Finally, as Lane Kenworthy argues in Chapter 1.2, full employment should be the priority target of the Federal Reserve, not just low rates of inflation. Looking back at Figure 1.1.1 in this chapter, we see that the longest period of relatively strong growth for families at the middle and lower end of the income distribution was in the mid–1990s through to 2000, when the unemployment rate was very low – even dipping below 4% for a time. Since the bargaining power (and therefore the compensation) of low- and middle-income workers are most affected by the unemployment rate, a government policy that emphasises the importance of low unemployment helps low- and middle-income families the most. Of course, this is especially relevant in the current moment, when job creation must be the top priority. Looking ahead, improving the living standards of low- and middle-income households needs to be established as a driving micro- *and* macroeconomic goal that shapes politics, policies and public debate alike.

Notes

[1] Data from Pikkety, T. and Saez, E. (2010) 'Income inequality in the United States', Table A3. Available at: http://elsa.berkeley.edu/~saez/TabFig2008.xls

[2] Data from Mishel, L., Bernstein, J. and Shierholz, H. (2009) *The state of working America 2008/2009*, Washington DC: Economic Policy Institute, Table 1.18.

[3] Whittaker, M. and Savage, L. (2011) 'Missing out: why ordinary workers are experiencing growth without gain', Resolution Foundation. Available at: http://www.resolutionfoundation.org/media/media/downloads/Missing_Out.pdf

[4] Data from Mishel et al (2009), op cit, Figure 1T.

[5] Data from Pikkety and Saez (2010), op cit, Table B2.

[6] Brewer, M. and Wren-Lewis, L. (2001) *Why did Britain's households get richer? Decomposing UK household income growth between 1968 and 2008–9*, London: Institute for Fiscal Studies analysis for Resolution Foundation.

[7] Mishel, L. (2011) 'Education is not the cure for high unemployment or for income inquality', Economic Policy Institute briefing paper. Available at: http://www.epi.org/publications/entry/education_is_not_the_cure_for_high_unemployment_or_for_income_inequality/

[8] Bivens, J. (2011) 'Failure by design: the story behind America's broken economy', Ithaca, NY: Cornell University Press.

[9] Gosling, A., Machin, S. and Meghir, C. (1999) 'The changing distribution of male wages in the UK', Institute for Fiscal Studies working paper series W98/9. Available at: http://www.ifs.org.uk/wps/wp9809.pdf

[10] Holmes, C. and Mayhew, K. (2012) *The changing shape of the UK job market and its implications for the bottom half of earners*, London: Resolution Foundation.

[11] Wilson, R., Homenidou, K. and Gambin, L. (2008) *Working futures 2007–2017*, London: UK Commission on Employment and Skills.

[12] Holmes, C. and Mayhew, K. (2012), op cit.

[13] Bivens, J. (2011), op cit.

[14] Western, B. and Rosenfeld, J. (2011) 'Unions, norms and the rise in American wage inequality'. Available at: http://www.wjh.harvard.edu/soc/faculty/western/pdfs/Unions_Norms_and_Wage_Inequality.pdf

Rising incomes and modest inequality: the high-employment route

Lane Kenworthy

During the period between the Second World War and the mid-1970s, the US enjoyed rapid economic growth, rising incomes for households across the distribution and a decline in income inequality. Since then, growth has continued, albeit at a slower pace. But, as Larry Mishel and Heidi Shierholz document in Chapter 1.1, the incomes of households at the middle and bottom have risen much less rapidly, both in an absolute sense and relative to the incomes of those at the top.

This presents a challenge to social democrats. If growth no longer secures rising living standards for low- and middle-income households, is there anything else that can be done to ensure that these families thrive in the modern economy? In this chapter, I first explore why strategies that worked in the past – namely, wage growth – may no longer work in the future. I then recommend an alternative: high employment. High employment would both raise household earnings and shore up the financing of redistributive government transfer programmes. High employment is not, however, a silver bullet, and I conclude by highlighting other policies that would complement and reinforce its benefits.

The broken link between economic growth and wages

During the early post-war decades, much of the growth in incomes for working-age Americans came from rising wages, which increased more or less in line with the growth of the economy. As Mishel and Shierholz (Chapter 1.1) show, that link has been severed for those in the lower half of the wage distribution.[1] Since the 1970s, real wages in the bottom half have barely budged.

The key to rising wages during the post-war golden age was that many US firms faced limited product market competition, limited pressure from shareholders to maximise near-term profits and significant pressure from unions (or the threat of unions) to pass on a 'fair' share of profits to employees. Each of these three institutional features is gone, and it is unlikely that they will return. Moreover, a host of additional developments now push against wage growth: technological change, stagnant educational attainment, the shift of employment from manufacturing to services, a more general trend away from middle-paying jobs, a rise in less-skilled immigration, growing prevalence of winner-take-all labour markets, a shift towards pay for performance and minimum wage decline.

The story is somewhat different in the UK. Real wages in the lower half rose between 1977 and 2003. But after that, the increase stopped, despite strong economic growth up to 2008. Resolution Foundation analysis suggests that the wages of a typical full-time male worker in the low- to middle-income group would be lower in 2020 than at their peak in 2003, even assuming that the economy returns to steady economic growth after 2017.[2] Will the UK's pay trend replicate what has happened in the US? It is too soon to tell, but given the similarity in labour markets and other economic institutions, it would not be surprising to see patterns in the US mirrored in the UK unless policymakers deliberately seek to alter the current trajectory.

Rising market inequality

The US and the UK have both experienced sharply rising income inequality, with more and more of the economic growth going to those at or near the top.[3] Although this trend is not unique to these two countries, it has been especially pronounced in them.

There are a number of factors at play here. As Figure 1.1.4 in Chapter 1.1 shows, inequality in the distribution of wages has been rising for some time now. This is extended and accentuated by family trends. Delayed marriage and frequent divorce result in lots of single-adult households. There is also evidence in the US and the UK of increasing 'marital homogamy' – higher-skilled, higher-earning people coupling with others like them. The net effect of this is to create many households with two earners and many with no earners or just one, and that in turn results in greater inequality of earnings and incomes between households. At the top, shifts in corporate governance, deregulation, financial innovations, rising stock prices and other developments have contributed to outsized growth in pay and capital gains. Some of these causes of rising market inequality are potentially amenable to policy intervention, but an appropriate and workable fix is far from straightforward.

Redistributive mechanisms are under increasing pressure

A key strategy for tackling rising market inequality in recent years has been to redistribute money to households. Indeed, many developed countries have increased the amounts of redistribution through their taxation and transfer systems.[4]

However, for the majority of countries, this increase has not been sufficient to offset the rise in market inequality, so post-tax, post-transfer inequality has increased too. And despite their increasingly important role in supporting the household incomes of low earners, redistributive measures face new pressures. Both taxes and transfers can redistribute. But, as the first chart in Figure 1.2.1 shows, in practice, transfers do most (if not all) of the work. In most rich countries, the overall tax system is roughly proportional: people at various points in the income distribution pay a similar share of their market income in taxes. In the US, for instance, taxes on personal and corporate income are progressive, but they only represent 14% of gross domestic product (GDP). Their progressivity is largely offset by regressive consumption and payroll taxes, which total 12% of GDP.

Taxes, though, provide the funds for the transfers that achieve the bulk of the inequality reduction. The second chart in Figure 1.2.1 shows a strong positive association across countries between tax revenues as a share of GDP and the amount of redistribution achieved via government transfers.

The problem is this: the economic recession has strained government finances in a number of rich countries. For example, the UK government's austerity programme has led to £2.5 billion of cuts to tax credits for low- to middle-income families in 2012/13. Population ageing will prove an even bigger challenge, raising the costs of pay-as-you-go pension systems and government-funded health care. A growing share of government revenues will need to go to the elderly, leaving less available for countering wage stagnation and rising market inequality.

A high-employment route

If government revenue from taxes will be stretched to meet the growing demands of an ageing population, where will the additional money come from to boost the incomes of low- and middle-income households? In the 1960s and 1970s, the standard response would have been to increase tax rates. The US has ample room to raise tax rates. In 2007, US tax revenues were just 28% of GDP, and total (tax plus

Figure 1.2.1: Taxes, transfers and inequality reduction, circa 2000

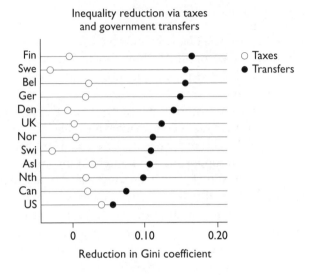

Inequality reduction via taxes
and government transfers

Reduction in Gini coefficient

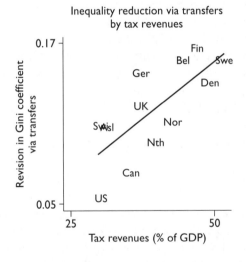

Inequality reduction via transfers
by tax revenues

Source: L. Kenworthy (2011) *Progress for the Poor*, Oxford: Oxford University Press, Figures 8.3 and 8.4, using Luxembourg Income Study and Organisation for Economic Co-operation and Development (OECD) data.
Key: Asl = Australia; Bel = Belgium; Can = Canada; Den = Denmark; Fin = Finland; Ger = Germany; Net = Netherlands; Nor = Norway; Swe = Sweden; Swi = Switzerland; UK = United Kingdom; US = United States

non-tax) government revenues were 34%. Indeed, as Tamara Draut notes in Chapter 3.1, tax rates in the US have dropped over the last half-century, with tax revenues holding constant as a share of GDP only because the tax base has been widened. In the UK, tax revenues were 36% of GDP in 2007. This, too, is well below the levels of a number of other rich nations. In Denmark and Sweden, for instance, tax revenues in 2007 were 48–49% of GDP and total government revenues were 54–55%. This does not appear to have damaged these countries' economies.[5] However, capital mobility and public receptivity to anti-tax rhetoric make the politics of raising taxes extremely challenging. This is where employment comes in. Beyond its benefits to individuals,[6] employment can contribute to rising incomes and modest inequality.[7] First, people who move from government benefits into work tend to improve their income, at least in the long run. That helps with income growth. Second, because earnings from employment are taxed, a rising employment rate increases tax revenues without requiring an increase in tax rates. High employment can thereby help to generate the revenues needed to fund transfers that offset stagnant wages and rising market inequality. Third, high employment also eases the fiscal crunch by reducing the number of people fully or heavily reliant on government benefits.

How to do it

The UK came through the depths of the recent recession with employment rates remaining higher than expected given previous experiences during the 1980s' and 1990s' downturns.[8] That said, it may be some time before employment returns to pre-recession levels. And there is no guarantee that the UK will continue its upward trajectory. Indeed, it could well slip into the kind of employment stagnation that befell the US from 2000 to 2007, with growing numbers forced into underemployment. Furthermore, as Figure 1.2.2 shows, US and UK employment rates were well below those of the leading affluent countries even before the economic crisis hit in 2008. Employment rates for prime-working-age (25 to 54) men probably cannot go up much further. But among prime-working-age women and particularly among the near-elderly (55 to 64), both male and female, there is considerable room for increase.

For several decades now, the US has pursued a market liberal approach to employment growth: a low wage floor, very limited labour market regulations, relatively stingy government benefits, comparatively low taxes, steady deregulation of product markets and limited support for retraining, job placement and work–family balance. Up to the turn of the century, the 'great American jobs machine' was comparatively successful, with the US one of the rich world's leaders in raising its employment rate. But in the 2000s, the bloom fell off the rose, as

Figure 1.2.2: Employment rates by sex and age group, 2007

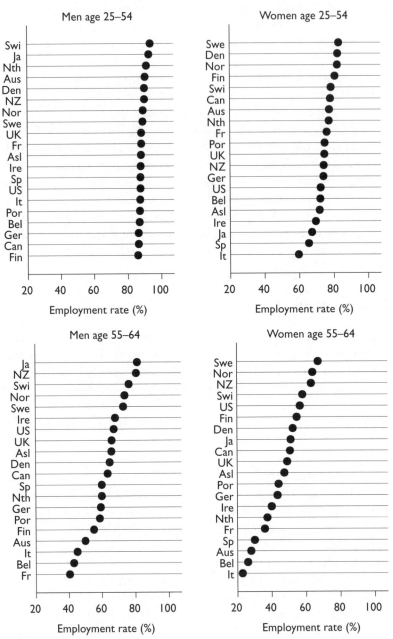

Source: Author's analysis of OECD data
Key: Asl = Australia; Aus = Austria; Bel = Belgium; Can = Canada; Den = Denmark;
Fin = Finland; Fra = France; Ger = Germany; Ire = Ireland; It = Italy; Ja = Japan;
Net = Netherlands; Nor = Norway; NZ = New Zealand; Por = Portugal; Sp = Spain;
Swe = Sweden; Swi = Switzerland; UK = United Kingdom; US = United States

Figure 1.2.3: Employment rates, age 25 to 64, 1979–2010

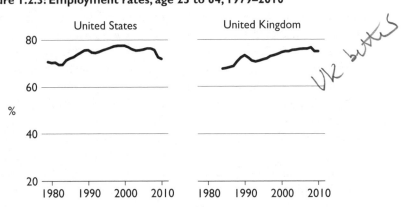

Source: Author's analysis of OECD data

Figure 1.2.3 indicates.[9] The early years of recovery after the 2001 recession featured feeble job growth, and things did not improve much after that. By the peak year (2007), the employment rate had not yet recovered to its 2000 level.[10]

During the debate surrounding the OECD's early-1990s' 'jobs study',[11] the virtue of the American model was seen as its ability to create lots of jobs. Whether that success was confined to a specific historical period or was always something of a chimera, it now seems clear that more is needed.

First, adequate demand is essential. Once it finally emerges from the aftermath of the great recession, the US may struggle in the absence of a 1990s- or 2000s-style stock market or housing bubble to fuel consumer spending. Rising living standards in developing nations should help by boosting exports, and government job creation can enhance domestic demand (see later); but this is a significant question mark going forward.

Second, early education is a clear winner. It has been shown that lowering the cost of childcare produces a significant increase in the employment of married mothers, with even larger effects for single mothers.[12] Beyond this economic case, evidence is mounting that good, affordable childcare contributes to equality of opportunity, improved life chances for those at the bottom, social mobility, and perhaps also equality of outcomes.[13]

Historically, social policy has been developed around an assumed male breadwinner/female carer model, with the result that social service provision for children or the elderly was underdeveloped. The Nordic countries began to prioritise family services in the 1970s, whereas governments in the US and the UK preferred to stimulate the market and subsidise care provision through tax deductions. The Labour administrations of 1997–2010 did much to address market failures in childcare, but their legacy is fragile. The new Coalition government reduced support for childcare in 2011 and it remains the case that childcare provision in the UK is patchy, expensive and inflexible. Still, it is much better than in the US.

Third, improvement in elementary, secondary and tertiary schooling is needed.[14] Just three-quarters of a typical American cohort complete high school, and the share getting a four-year college degree has risen only slightly since the late 1970s. Fourth, the US should sharply expand provision of individualised assistance for those who struggle in the labour market. This is expensive, but it helps.[15] Fifth, government can subsidise private sector job growth and create public sector jobs. One candidate is green jobs.[16] Another is helping/caring services, including the provision of information. Sixth, efforts to make low-end jobs pay well enough to be attractive have been inconsistent. Key tools include the statutory minimum wage and the Earned Income Tax Credit.[17] I discuss these later.

The New Labour governments embraced several of these approaches – childcare, reform of schools, individualised assistance in training and job search, and making work pay – albeit on a somewhat limited scale. Those efforts were a clear step in the right direction, and they made a difference.[18] Continuing, enhancing and improving them is likely to boost employment further. But as we have already seen, New Labour's positive legacy is threatened on several fronts as a result of the new government's decision to eliminate the public deficit in a single parliament.

How much additional revenue?

Can higher employment really generate enough tax revenues to fund the government transfers needed to ensure decent incomes and moderate income inequality? It is impossible to be certain, but I think there are grounds for optimism.[19] When a person shifts from being non-employed or a benefit recipient or employed off-the-books to a job in the formal sector, income and payroll tax receipts increase. Consumption tax revenues may also rise. And some people will move up to higher-paying positions, generating further additional tax revenues.

Here is a back-of-the-envelope calculation for the US: in 2007, just before the recession, taxes on income and payroll totalled about 18% of GDP. If the US were to increase its employment-to-population ratio[20] by about one sixth, from 62% to 72%, revenues from income and payroll taxes might rise by two or three percentage points of GDP. That could finance a very large expansion of the Earned Income Tax Credit (see later); or it could fund a Nordic-style family policy.[21] If there were additional revenue from consumption taxes and reduced spending on some types of transfer payments (unemployment compensation, social assistance, disability), the fiscal benefit would be even larger.

A future of lousy jobs?

In an ideal world, everyone would have high-quality, well-paid employment. That, however, is not going to happen. Even if more and better education helps to push the quality mix of new jobs in a favourable direction, we must accept that a significant share of employment growth will be in low-end services. These are jobs that require limited schooling and in which productivity improvement is difficult – cleaning, caring, assisting and so on. We ought to embrace low-end service employment and figure out how to make it better.

This brings me back to wages. Despite the breakdown of the relationship between pay and economic growth, we should not abandon efforts to increase wages. Here, I see five complementary solutions. The first is high employment itself. A tight labour market – low unemployment, often referred to as 'full employment' – tends to push wages up. We can see this in the one and only period since the 1970s in which real wages in the bottom half of the US distribution have increased: the late 1990s. The key factor seems to have been an unemployment rate that got as low as 4%.[22] A high employment rate does not guarantee a low unemployment rate, but it makes it more likely.

It would be good to repeat the late 1990s' experience. But while it is within the power of policymakers to achieve full employment, there is a good chance they will not do so. If and when the US gets near 4% unemployment again, I suspect the Federal Reserve will be less willing than it was in the late 1990s to resist stepping on the brakes. The Federal Reserve chair at that time, Alan Greenspan, held interest rates low despite opposition from other Federal Reserve board members, who were concerned about potential inflationary consequences of rapid growth, rising wages and the internet stock market bubble. Greenspan took this stance in part because his belief in the self-correcting nature of markets led him to worry less than others about the bubble. In light of the painful consequences of the 2000s' real estate bubble, I doubt that the Federal Reserve will take that approach again for some time.

A second solution for wages is unions. Unionisation is a tried-and-true strategy for improving pay. Unions have been slow to organise low-end services, but there have been some successes, as Eileen Appelbaum and Carrie Leana show in Chapter 2.1. It would be good to see more of this kind of work in both countries.

A third solution is public employment. Public sector jobs tend to have better pay than comparable private sector ones. This has been a key element of the Nordic countries' success in bolstering the incomes of people in low-end service positions. Expansion of childcare, early education, care for the elderly, the ill and the disabled, and a host of other low-end services can occur partly via public employment.

A fourth solution is subsidies to boost household incomes. Here, the UK and the US have existing programmes, the Working Tax Credit and the Earned Income Tax Credit, on which to build (discussed by Daniel Gitterman in Chapter 2.4).[23] In the US, the Earned Income Tax Credit currently boosts the incomes mainly of households near the bottom of the distribution. There is a good case for expanding the credit to reach those further up the scale. In the UK, the greater generosity of out-of-work benefits means that the work incentives of the Working Tax Credit, particularly for second earners, can be rather weak. Despite the government's commitment to make work pay, it appears that the newly designed Universal Credit will not significantly improve work incentives for second earners and may, in fact, make things worse for many families.[24]

A fifth solution is the statutory minimum wage. The US ought to follow the UK in establishing an independent commission to determine when and by how much the minimum wage should be increased. In the US, the federal minimum wage is too low, and state-mandated levels, though they help, in many instances do not suffice to bring it up to where it ought to be. Even in the UK, the minimum wage has not fully kept up with inflation. In real terms, today's minimum wage is lower than it was in 2004.[25]

In Chapter 2.2, Francoise Carré and James Heintz draw our attention to the importance of work conditions alongside pay. Will a high-employment strategy help shore up the welfare state, secure decent incomes for the bottom half, maintain an acceptable level of inequality and yet leave a significant portion of the population working in drudgery? It need not turn out that way. There is a limit to the amount of stimulation that some low-end jobs will ever be able to provide. But most could do better, and efforts to figure out how and to push firms in that direction are well worth undertaking. Indeed, there is good reason to favour direct action to improve working conditions in *all* jobs, instead of assuming that higher-skilled, better-paying positions – the kind we surely would like to have more of – will necessarily feature a decent quality of work life.

One piece of the puzzle

A generation ago it was fairly common on the centre-left to view freedom from work ('decommodification') as an integral element of the good society. In the 1990s, the tide began to turn in favour of employment, activation and the social investment state. Now, in the aftermath of rising inequality, stagnant relative poverty rates and a severe economic crisis, this in turn is itself facing questioning and criticism.[26]

That is healthy. It is always wise to rethink and re-examine. My own view, though, is that the case for a high-employment path is stronger than ever. The obstacles to rising incomes and modest inequality are formidable. High employment is only part of the answer. But it is an important part.

Notes

[1] See also Mishel, L., Bernstein, J. and Shierholz, H. (2009) *The state of working America*, Washington DC: Economic Policy Institute; Plunkett, J. (2011) 'Growth without gain? The faltering living standards of people on low-to-middle incomes', Resolution Foundation, available at: http://www.resolutionfoundation.org/media/media/downloads/Growth_without_gain_-_Web.pdf; and Whittaker, M. and Savage, L. (2011) 'Missing out: why ordinary workers are experiencing growth without gain', Resolution Foundation, available at: http://www.resolutionfoundation.org/media/media/downloads/Missing_Out.pdf

[2] The Resolution Foundation (2012) *Essential guide to squeezed Britain: The annual audit of low to middle income households*, London: The Resolution Foundation.

[3] Atkinson, A.B., Piketty, T. and Saez, E. (2009) 'Top incomes in the long run of history', Working Paper 15408, National Bureau of Economic Research.

[4] Kenworthy, L. and Pontusson, J. (2005) 'Rising inequality and the politics of redistribution in affluent countries', *Perspectives on Politics*, vol 3, no 3, pp 449-71.

[5] Kenworthy, L. (2011) 'Is heavy taxation bad for the economy?', Consider the Evidence. Available at: http://considertheevidence.net/2011/05/22/is-heavy-taxation-bad-for-the-economy

[6] Employment imposes regularity and discipline on people's lives. It can be a source of mental stimulation. It helps to fulfill the widespread desire to contribute to, and be integrated with, the larger society. It contributes to identity and self-esteem. With family and neighbourhood ties weakening, it is an increasingly important site of social interaction.

[7] Ferrera, M., Hemerijck, A. and Rhodes, M. (2000) 'The future of social Europe: recasting work and welfare in the new economy', report prepared for the Portuguese Presidency of the European Union, http://www.zoot.unifi. it/relazioni-internazionali-studi-europei/upload/sub/Ferrera_Hemerijck_ Rhodes.pdf; Scharpf, F. and Schmidt, V. (eds) (2000) *Welfare and work in the open economy*, Oxford: Oxford University Press; Esping-Andersen, G., Gallie, D., Hemerijck, A. and Myles, J. (2002) *Why we need a new welfare state*, Oxford: Oxford University Press; Kenworthy, L. (2004) *Egalitarian capitalism*, New York, NY: Russell Sage Foundation; OECD (2006) *Employment outlook: boosting jobs and incomes,* Paris: OECD; Kenworthy, L. (2008) *Jobs with equality*, Oxford: Oxford University Press; Kenworthy, L. (2009) 'The high-employment route to low inequality', *Challenge*, vol 52, no 5, pp 77-99.

[8] Gregg, P. and Wadsworth, J. (eds) (2010) *The labour market in winter: the state of working Britain,* Oxford: Oxford University Press.

[9] Freeman, R.B. and Rodgers, W.M. (2005) 'The weak jobs recovery: whatever happened to "the great American jobs machine"?', Federal Reserve Bank of New York, *Economic Policy Review*, vol 11, no 1, pp 3-18; Gordon, R. (2010) 'Okun's Law and productivity innovations', *American Economic Review Papers and Proceedings* vol 100, pp 11-15; Kenworthy, L. (2011) 'The late American jobs machine', Consider the Evidence, available at: http://considertheevidence. net/2011/09/13/the-late-american-jobs-machine

[10] Rising employment is particularly important for those at the low end of the labour market. Here, too, the 2000s' upturn was a disappointment. In working-age households in the bottom quartile of the income distribution, average employment hours failed to rise at all. See Kenworthy, L. and Bentele, K. (2011) 'How trickle down can fail: the U.S. case', in Kenworthy, L. (ed) *Progress for the poor*, Oxford: Oxford University Press, ch 3.

[11] OECD (1994) *The OECD jobs study,* Paris: OECD.

[12] Blau, D. (2001) *The child care problem. an economic analysis*, New York, NY: Russell Sage Foundation.

[13] Kenworthy (2008), op cit, ch 10; Esping-Andersen, G. (2009) *The incomplete revolution,* Cambridge: Polity Press; Cunha, F. and Heckman, J.J. (2010) 'Investing in our young people', Working Paper 16201, National Bureau of Economic Research; OECD (2011) *Doing better for families,* Paris: OECD.

---

[14] Kenworthy, L. (2011) 'Two and a half cheers for education', in Cramme, O. and Diamond, P. (eds) *After the third way: the future of social democracy in Europe*, London: I.B. Taurus.

[15] Ben-Galim, D. and Sachraida Dal, A. (eds) (2009) 'Now it's personal: learning from welfare-to-work approaches around the world', Institute for Public Policy Research. Available at: http://www.ippr.org/publications/55/1797/now-its-personal-the-new-landscape-of-welfare-to-work

[16] Apollo Alliance (2008) 'Creating green-collar jobs in America's cities', Center for American Progress and Center on Wisconsin Strategy. Available at: http://www.americanprogress.org/issues/2008/03/pdf/green_collar_jobs.pdf

[17] Kenworthy, L. (2009) 'Reducing inequality: boosting incomes in the bottom half', Consider the Evidence. Available at: http://considertheevidence.net/2009/04/16/reducing-inequality-boosting-incomes-in-the-bottom-half

[18] Waldfogel, J. (2010) *Britain's war on poverty*, New York, NY: Russell Sage Foundation, ch 2; Finn, D. and Schulte, B. (2008) '"Employment first": activating the British welfare state', in Eichhorst, W., Kaufmann, O. and Konle-Seidl, R. (eds) *Bringing the jobless into work?*, New York, NY: Springer.

[19] For a fuller discussion, see Kenworthy (2009), op cit, pp 289–91.

[20] All employed persons as a share of the total population. This is different from the data shown in Figure 1.2.3, which are for employed persons age 25–64 as a share of the population age 25–64.

[21] The difference between what the US currently spends on child payments and allowances, parental leave benefits, and child care support versus what Denmark and Sweden spend is 2–3% of GDP. See OECD (2011) op cit, Figure 1.11.

[22] Bernstein, J. and Baker, D. (2003) *The benefits of full employment*, Washington D.C.: Economic Policy Institute.

[23] See also Kenworthy (2008), op cit, ch 7; Kenworthy, L. (2011) *Progress for the poor*, Oxford: Oxford University Press, ch 5.

[24] Hirsch, D. (2011) *Tackling the adequacy trap: earnings, incomes and work incentives under the Universal Credit*, London: Resolution Foundation.

[25] Manning, A. (2012) *Minimum wage: maximum impact*, London: Resolution Foundation.

[26] Morel, N., Palier, B. and Palme, J. (eds) (2009) *What future for social investment?*, Stockholm: Institute for Futures Studies; Cantillon, B. (2010) 'Disambiguating Lisbon: growth, employment and social inclusion in the investment state',

Working Paper 10-07, Centre for Social Policy, University of Antwerp; McTernan, M. (ed) (2011) *Social progress in the 21st century: social investment, labour market reform, and intergenerational equity*, London: Policy Network.

Section 2

Policy lessons: creating quality work, raising incomes and building greater economic security

Creating quality work

Improving job quality in low-paid jobs: care workers in the US

Eileen Appelbaum and Carrie Leana

Around the seminar rooms of London and Washington, there is much talk about the need for an industrial strategy to support sectors of the economy with the most potential for employment growth. Often, the focus of these discussions is infrastructure investment and green jobs. Below the surface, however, is a nagging concern on the part of policymakers about the sharp decline in the employment-to-population ratio of men in their prime working years. Although this development preceded the recent recession, it was greatly exacerbated by it.

In part, the decline can be explained by the dominance of women in the US industries exhibiting the strongest growth in payroll employment in the years prior to the downturn – education and health services.[1] Even as the recession led to a collapse of employment in the rest of the economy, privately provided education and health services added 844,000 jobs. Between December 2007 and April 2011, employment in education and health services increased by 7% as the sector added more than 1.3 million jobs. Home health care jobs alone grew by 20%. Overall, paraprofessional jobs in health care are predicted to grow three times faster than all other occupations in the years to come.[2]

These jobs are unattractive to men because of the very low wages paid – too low to support a family – but also because of cultural stereotypes. The marginalised status of occupations in paraprofessional health care in terms of wages, benefits and employment law protections is a legacy of the politics of race and gender in the US as it applied to work performed in what was viewed as the domestic sphere. In the late 19th and early 20th centuries, domestic work was viewed as women's work – good marital training for women – and outside the sphere of production. In the New Deal of the 1930s, the economic interests of the South shaped the legal framework surrounding domestic service. Unwilling to expand the political or economic power of African-Americans and seeking to maintain an inexpensive supply of labour,

Table 2.1.1: Fifteen occupations with largest projected US job growth, 2008–2018

2008 National Employment Matrix Occupation Code		Median annual wage quartile 2008	Per cent female 2010	Per cent black 2010	Per cent Hispanic 2010
1.	Registered nurses	VH	91.0	12.0	4.9
2.	**Home health aides**	**VL**	**88.2**	**34.6**	**14.7**
3.	Customer service representatives	L	66.6	17.5	15.2
4.	Combined food preparation and serving workers, including fast food	VL	61.3	12.8	16.6
5.	**Personal and home care aides**	**VL**	**86.1**	**23.8**	**17.6**
6.	Retail salespersons	VL	51.0	11.3	13.7
7.	Office clerks, general	L	84.2	13.0	15.6
8.	Accountants and auditors	VH	60.1	8.6	5.8
9.	**Nursing aides, orderlies and attendants**	**L**	**88.2**	**34.6**	**14.7**
10.	Post-secondary teachers	VH	45.9	6.3	5.0
11.	Construction labourers	L	2.7	9.0	43.1
12.	Elementary school teachers, except special education	H	81.8	9.3	7.3
13.	Truck drivers, heavy and tractor-trailer	H	4.6	13.6	17.5
14.	Landscaping and grounds-keeping workers	L	N/A	N/A	N/A
15.	Bookkeeping, accounting and auditing clerks	H	90.0	6.5	8.8

Notes: VH = very high, H = high, L = low and VL = very low. These letters refer to the wage quartile in which the occupation falls. Thus, VL is an occupation whose median wage falls at or below the 25th percentile in the US wage distribution.

Source: US Department of Labor, US Bureau of Labor Statistics, 'Employment Projections Program' (available at: www.bls.gov/emp/ep_table_104.htm) and 'Employed Persons by Detailed Occupation, Sex, Race and Hispanic or Latino Ethnicity' (available at: www.bls.gov/cps/cpsaat11.pdf).

Southern politicians worked to exclude domestic service (and farm labour) from the New Deal labour reforms.

The historical legacy that shapes the US care market today may be unique to the country, but there are some strikingly similar labour market trends in the UK. Employment in education and health and social care has been growing in the UK over the last decade and demand for care and support is projected to rise sharply in the coming years just as it is in the US.[3]

Scenario work by the Department of Health suggests that an ageing population and medical advances will expand the care workforce in England to 2.6 million people by 2025 – the equivalent of 3.1 million jobs – of which a third will be personal assistant or directly employed care worker roles. Even in a more conservative scenario, this means that the care sector is expanding rapidly at a time when many other sectors – particularly those that have historically been dominated by men – are in decline.

These shifting patterns of growth across different sectors of the economy must be reflected in the industrial strategies of both nations as our governments search out ways of kick-starting an economic recovery. And that means focusing on what can be termed 'low productivity' sectors such as health and social care, as much as 'high productivity' knowledge and technology occupations: these are sectors that will employ growing numbers of low and modest earners, who rely on their work to support their families. Starting with this premise, we offer here an overview of what the latest US research and practice tells us about how to invest in job quality in this poorly understood sector.

This chapter focuses on the paid workforce in social care, rather than the huge army of unpaid carers – mostly family members – who play such a vital role in both countries. Workforce issues have historically been marginalised in debates in the UK. Even with a recent surge of interest – see, for example, the publication of a workforce development strategy[4] and a forthcoming framework for personal assistants[5] – it is difficult to see how a policy agenda that aims to reduce regulation, coupled with major austerity measures, will lift care work from being a 'Cinderella profession encumbered with negativity'[6] to a career of positive choice that provides people with job satisfaction and economic security.

Drawing on American research, this chapter argues that an industrial strategy for the health and social care sector will need concrete policies that raise wages, improve working conditions and provide opportunities for career mobility, as well as initiatives to increase the dignity of the paraprofessional health care workers who provide hands-on, non-medical care services – personal or home care aides, home health aides and certified nursing assistants and orderlies. These changes are essential for maintaining a vibrant middle class.

A Cinderella workforce

While health care is organised very differently in the US and the UK, both countries provide personal and social care via a mixed economy, where providers operate in either the government or the voluntary or private sector, and where care is paid for by a combination of means-tested publicly funded support and individual contributions. In addition, informal unpaid care shores up a chronically underfunded sector in both countries.[7]

Looking at the paid workforce within this mixed economy of care in the US, jobs are treated as unskilled work, with little regard for the knowledge, communication skills and emotional requirements of providing quality care. Training is mostly informal and 'on the job', with most states requiring workers to complete just 75 hours of formal training. Furthermore, as Table 2.1.1 shows, these are also very low-wage jobs, with pay falling into the bottom quartile of earnings. Employer-paid health insurance and pension schemes – indicators of job quality in the US – are unusual, with less than half of home health aides and home care aides having access to such a scheme. Indeed, a third of these workers have no health insurance at all.

While English care workers do not need to pay for health insurance, their job quality is worryingly low for a sector projected to grow so significantly in coming years. It is low paid and dominated by women, who undertake between 85% and 95% of all direct care and support-providing jobs in England. In 2009, median gross hourly pay for care workers varied between sectors but no one was well paid, and jobs offering the minimum wage or near this are common. The £6.00 an hour paid in 2010 to carers in the private sector was 50 pence less than the median pay for supermarket checkout workers.[8] One in eight low-paid jobs are in the health and social care sector,[9] and the Low Pay Commission has repeatedly expressed a concern that social care budgets are failing to reflect minimum wage requirements.[10]

The UK may do better than the US at ensuring its 1.75 million care workers have basic work supports, such as paid sick leave and annual holiday allowances. Many of those who provide hands-on care are subject to zero hours contracts, which provide little security or opportunity for progression. Despite growing concern with the quality of care provided to vulnerable adults and several high-profile abuse scandals, limited attention is paid to workforce conditions in the UK and how they affect the care provided.

At the same time as a rapid expansion in the *number* of jobs available, the *nature* of work in the health and social care sector is changing. Domiciliary or home-based care work is growing faster than institution-based care in both countries: for example, by 2018, 800,000 of the projected 1.3 million paraprofessional care positions in the US will be in home-based care. And consumer-directed care – better known as personalisation or self-directed support in the UK – whereby people receive Direct Payments from which they pay for the costs of their care, is also growing rapidly. There were 168,000 unregulated personal assistants in England in 2010, and this is predicted to rise to 722,000 in 2025, meaning greater numbers of workers will be employed directly by those for whom they care.[11]

While these developments may have positive outcomes for many people wishing to be cared for at home, they have more ambiguous implications for the workforce unless there are changes to the regulatory and cultural environment of the sector. Care work that is carried out behind people's front doors is hard to monitor. Direct Payment recipients who are unfamiliar with the responsibilities of being an employer may not enforce the rights of their workers. A fragmented workforce makes individual, structured and organised approaches to career development extremely challenging.

In the light of these working conditions, it is hardly surprising that turnover is a long-standing problem in this industry. The persistent high rate of turnover in many areas is a critical and unresolved factor contributing to staff shortages, poor-quality care and unnecessary costs of long-term care. A 2002 national survey of US nursing homes found annual turnover rates among certified nursing assistants to be greater than 70% and average vacancy rates to be almost 12%.[12] These are far higher than the equivalent figures in England, but at 3.1%, vacancy rates in social care are still twice the level for all industrial, commercial and public sector activities. About one in four English care workers leave their jobs each year, with turnover being more pronounced among lower-paid staff than managers.[13]

Improving job quality in an era of home-based care

So it is clear that domiciliary care is set to rise faster than institution-based care: personal and home care aides and home health aides are the third- and fourth-fastest growing detailed occupations in the US.[14] Furthermore, an increasing proportion of state funding for social care is being channelled into 'consumer-directed' care. This growth in home-based care workers is an important development for the personalisation agenda, but it makes it harder than ever to regulate and improve job quality.

In 2011, a broad-based US coalition that included the National Domestic Workers Alliance, unions working to organise direct care workers, the National Employment Law Project, advocates for a higher minimum wage or for paid sick days, and numerous community groups and non-governmental organisations (NGOs) launched a major initiative – Caring Across Generations – to improve the quality of work for direct care workers working in people's private households.

The goal of this coalition is to pass comprehensive legislation to address the multiple disadvantages of care workers in health services and to improve clients' access to affordable quality care. Reforming employment law so that personal and home care workers are covered by wage and hour laws, occupational health and safety laws, family and medical leave laws, and union organising rules is fundamental to changing the policy framework for these workers and overcoming their marginalisation in the labour market. Beyond these legislative changes, the coalition is campaigning for a series of other improvements, two of which are particularly pertinent to the UK situation.

Workforce intermediaries

There is a great deal of work going into creating workforce intermediaries – organisations that aggregate workers and provide benefits to them and care recipients. Much of this work takes inspiration from earlier organising efforts in California by the Service Employees International Union (SEIU) – one of the largest unions in the US. The SEIU's work showed how intermediaries can make it easier for workers to reach fair pay agreements with states. They can also provide other services to both consumers and workers, such as access to background checks, worker registries and training. Our experience in the US indicates that incentives are needed – such as training opportunities, systems to provide backup in case of an emergency, worker screening and fiscal intermediary services – to attract privately paid workers, hired directly by care recipients or their families, to join such intermediaries.

States where intermediaries have been successfully set up, such as California, show that they not only improve working conditions for direct care workers, but also help families to access state and federal funding for which they are eligible. Research by Candace Howes into the Californian initiative documents a near doubling of wages for home care workers, an increase in both the number of workers and the number of consumers served by the programme, and a decline in various measures of turnover.[15]

The labour movement has successfully extended this model to provide basic labour protections to home care workers in eight states and to family day care providers – known as childminders in the UK – in 10 states. The Caring Across Generations coalition is now campaigning for states to be required to set up intermediaries, and enable workers to bargain with the state if a majority so chooses.

Career ladders and training

The second campaign area of potential interest to UK readers is the focus on training and career ladders for personal and home care workers – which are currently sorely lacking on both sides of the Atlantic. Here in the US, Caring Across Generations is pushing for a minimum national training standard, which would apply to all workers providing care paid for by state funding. This standard would increase the federal requirement for entry training for home health aides from 75 to 150 hours, as well as making training costs for home care workers eligible for reimbursement from the government, as they are for nursing home workers.

Given that one in five domiciliary care agencies did not meet the qualifications-related National Minimum Standards in England, there is much work to be done in the UK. Recent calls by Skills for Care to link training to remuneration frameworks are welcome and should be pursued. There is also campaigning work going on in the US to establish clearly articulated home care career pathways by defining a national Personal and Home Care Aide credential. Much more work is needed in the US to build a rationalised system that builds formally from one level of training to the next, with certifications for each that are transportable across settings and employers. The new Qualification and Credit Framework in England may have much to offer here but it needs to be evaluated.

Employer practice

Despite a shift towards home-based care in recent years, much long-term care continues to be provided in sometimes dismal institutional settings. In the UK and the US alike, serious concerns about quality persist,[16] notwithstanding improvements in clinical care in nursing homes over the last two decades. Addressing the needs of workers in care homes will continue to be an important priority, even with the growth in home-based provision.

There is a growing body of evidence from US research into working practices in care homes about how care quality can be improved. In particular, there has been a groundswell of interest in the introduction of 'high-performance' work practices into this sector, as evidence shows that such practices are correlated with a broad array of desired outcomes, including not only better care, but also greater job attachment and satisfaction.[17]

For example, the 'Better Jobs/Better Care' initiative set out to improve care quality by providing funding for interventions designed to improve the human resources practices in long-term care settings. These interventions centred variously on the quality of supervision to direct care workers, the addition of support personnel to advocate for workers and improve retention, establishing career paths, and instituting empowered work teams. The results of these studies are promising, with results generally in the expected direction, though sometimes mixed depending on the nature of the intervention. Programmes focused on enhancing the quality of supervision and peer mentoring have been shown to have some of the strongest positive effects on worker job attachment.[18]

It is likely that some of these mixed results arise as these kinds of interventions confront numerous challenges in the structure and the culture of the care sector as it stands today. For example, empowered work teams are trained and encouraged to respond to the individual needs of care recipients, but have difficulty doing this and completing other tasks. Job enhancements and other interventions may have limited impact, given the typical workloads of nursing assistants in long-term care facilities. Workers receive training, but have limited opportunities to increase wages or move into more responsible jobs, as the proportion of jobs that utilise these skills remains low.

Thus, while studies of the effects of interventions to improve work organisation and management practices suggest that improving human resource management can improve both job quality and the quality of care, the structural and institutional constraints on staffing and upward mobility in long-term care facilities continue to limit the effectiveness of these interventions.[19]

Conclusion

England spends £122 billion each year on health and social care – roughly a fifth of all public expenditure.[20] Much of this money is spent on the workforce, and yet much of care work remains a poorly paid profession with high turnover, low morale and few opportunities for advancement.

At the centre of any strategy for improving job quality in this sector is decent public sector investment. This may seem an obvious point, but it is a vital one given the cuts in public services on both sides of the Atlantic. Such cuts will make it hard for providers to meet even current levels of demand, let alone be ready for the future. It has serious implications for low and modest earners relying on jobs in the care sector for their economic well-being.

Beyond funding, as this chapter shows, better jobs will come from a steady focus on three priorities: improving employer practice, appropriate regulation and workforce organising. At a more fundamental level, both US and UK policymakers need to stop treating care as low-paid 'women's work' that is incidental to a family's income. More middle-class households than ever before will be relying on care jobs to raise their families and ensure a decent standard of living.

Improving job quality matters from a care quality perspective: the outcomes of care recipients are deeply intertwined with the fortunes of care workers. Morally, it is incumbent upon nations to care for the sick and elderly with dignity and respect. But improving job quality in the fields of health and social care is also critical for economic reasons. Social care is a growth sector and must be considered alongside green jobs and infrastructure investment when it comes to developing industrial and economic policy. Our care-giving infrastructure is as essential to a well-functioning economy – and as worthy of investment – as roads and bridges.

Notes

[1] In December 2007, at the start of the recent recession, the private (ie for-profit) education and health services sector was 77% female and employed 14.3 million women, in contrast to construction, which was 87% male and employed less than half as many (6.5 million) men. Authors' calculations from US Department of Labor, Bureau of Labor Statistics (2007) 'Historical Data on Employment, Hours and Earnings', Table B1 (available at: www.bls.gov/webapps/legacy/cesbtab1.htm) and Table B5 (available at: www.bls.gov/webapps/legacy/cesbtab5.htm).

[2] Dawson, S.L. (2007) *Recruitment and retention of paraprofessionals*, Institute of Medicine's Committee on the Future Health Care Workforce for Older Americans. See also Lacey, T. and Wright, B. (2009) 'Occupational employment projections to 2018', *Monthly Labor Review*, vol 13, no 211, pp 82–123. Available at: http://www.bls.gov/opub/mlr/2009/11/art5full.pdf

[3] Whittaker, M. (2011) *Missing out: why ordinary workers are experiencing growth without gain*, London: Resolution Foundation.

[4] Skills for Care (2011) 'Capable, confident, skilled – a workforce development strategy for people working, supporting and caring in adult social care'. Available at: http://www.skillsforcare.org.uk/wds/

[5] It has been reported that the Department of Health will produce a strategic framework for personal assistants. See, for example: http://www.communitycare.co.uk/Articles/2011/06/06/116947/the-employment-rights-of-personal-assistants.htm

[6] Skills for Care (2011) 'Adult social care workforce recruitment and retention strategy'. Available at: http://www.skillsforcare.org.uk/recruitmentandretentionstrategy/

[7] There are an estimated five million unpaid carers in England, 46% of whom are juggling their responsibilities at home with paid work. Of Americans, 61.6 million provided care at some point during 2009, with an estimated economic value of US$450 billion – an increase of US$75 billion since 2007, and a value equivalent to 3.2% of GDP.

[8] Eborall, C., Fenton, W. and Woodrow, S. (2010) *The state of the adult social care workforce in 2010*, Leeds: Skills for Care.

[9] Resolution Foundation (2010) 'Squeezed Britain: the 2010 audit of low-to-middle earners'. Available at: http://www.resolutionfoundation.org/publications/squeezed-britain-low-middle-earners-audit-2010/

[10] Low Pay Commission (2011) 'National minimum wage: the Low Pay Commission report 2011'. Available at: http://www.lowpay.gov.uk/lowpay/report/pdf/Revised_Report_PDF_with_April_date.PDF

[11] There were 114,500 recipients of direct payments in 2010, compared to 76,642 in 2007/08. See Eborall et al (2010), op cit.

[12] Decker, F., Gruhn, P., Matthews-Martin, L., Dollard, J., Tucker, A. and Bizette, L. (2003) *Results of the 2002 AHCA survey of nursing staff vacancy and turnover in nursing homes*, http://www.ahcancal.org/research_data/staffing/Documents/Vacancy_Turnover_Survey2002.pdf. More recent data show that the turnover rate among certified nursing assistants is about 65.6%, while the vacancy rate is 9.5%. There are an estimated 60,300 certified nursing assistant positions vacant, see American Health Care Association, Department of Research (2008) 'Report of findings, 2007 AHCA survey, nursing staff vacancy and turnover in nursing homes', Washington, DC. Available at: http://www.ahcancal.org/research_data/staffing/documents/vacancy_turnover_survey2007.pdf

---

[13] See Eborall et al (2010), op cit.

[14] US Department of Labor, Bureau of Labor Statistics (2010/11) 'Occupational outlook handbook, 2010–11 edition, overview of the 2008–18 projections', Table 1. Available at: www.bls.gov/oco/oco2003.htm#occupation_d

[15] See, for example, Howes, C. (2002) 'The impact of a large wage increase on the workforce stability of IHSS home care workers in San Francisco County', available at: http://www.pascenter.org/publications/publication_home.php?id=57; Howes, C. (2004) 'Upgrading California's home care workforce: the impact of political action and unionization', *The State of California Labor*, vol 4, pp 71–105; Howes, C. (2005) 'Living wages and retention of homecare workers in San Francisco', *Industrial Relations* vol 44, pp 139–163.

[16] Institute of Medicine (2001) *Crossing the quality chasm: a new health system for the 21st century*, Washington, DC: National Academies Press; Levinson, D.R. (2008) 'Trends in nursing home deficiencies and complaints', Inspector General Memorandum Report, OEI-02-08-00140, available at: http://oig.hhs.gov/oei/reports/oei-02-08-00140.pdf. See also Harrington, C., Carrillo, H., Blank, B.W. and O'Brian, T. (2010) 'Nursing facilities, staffing, residents, and facility deficiencies, 2004–2009', Department of Social and Behavioral Sciences, University of California. Available at: http://www.pascenter.org/documents/OSCAR_complete_2010.pdf

[17] Appelbaum, E., Bailey, T., Berg, P. and Kalleberg, A.L. (2000) *Manufacturing advantage: why high performance work systems pay off*, Ithaca, NY: Cornell University Press; see also Appelbaum, D., Gittell, J.H and Leana, C. (2008) 'High performance work practices and economic recovery', unpublished policy paper. Available at: www.employmentpolicy.org/topic/23/research/high-performance-work-practices-and-sustainable-economic-growth-0

[18] Morgan, J.C. and Konrad, T.R. (2008) 'A mixed-method evaluation of a workforce development intervention for nursing assistants in nursing homes: the case of WIN A STEP UP', *The Gerontologist* vol 48, no 1, pp 71–79. See also Kemper, P., Brannon, D., Barry T., Stott, A. and Heier, B. (2008) 'Implementation of the Better Jobs Better Care demonstration: lessons for long-term care workforce initiatives', *The Gerontologist*, vol 48, special issue no 1, pp 26–35.

[19] Wellin, C. (2007) 'Paid care-giving for older adults with serious or chronic illness: ethnographic perspectives and evidence', National Academies Center for Education on Research Evidence Related to Future Skill Demands, Panel on Skill Demands in Growing Service Sector Jobs, Washington, DC, 31 May–1 June. Available at: http://ilstu.academia.edu/ChrisWellin/Papers/1042343/

Paid_care-giving_for_older_adults_with_serious_or_chronic_illness_
Ethnographic_perspectives_evidence_and_implications_for_training

[20] Skills for Care (2011), op cit.

Employment change and economic vulnerability in the US

Françoise Carré and James Heintz

Since the 1980s, non-standard forms of employment have grown in the US, although detailed data documenting this trend have not always been consistently available. Drawing on earlier work,[1] we show here how non-standard employment produces economic vulnerability in a variety of ways: low and irregular earnings, underemployment and frequent unemployment or unstable labour market participation. Non-standard arrangements particularly affect women workers as a whole. They also disproportionately touch racial/ethnic minorities, primarily African-American workers and Hispanics. Non-citizens, that is, mostly recent immigrants, are also disproportionately affected by non-standard work. All of these groups may thus be exposed to economic risk through non-standard employment to a greater extent than other workers.

The US experience shows how these vulnerabilities are compounded by a lack of social protection schemes. UK workers may be able to depend on a National Health Service and more generous in-work and unemployment benefits, but even with these protections in place, non-standard employment leaves workers exposed to income instability and limited opportunities to save, which in turn makes household budgets and unexpected expenditures hard to manage. Significant cuts in tax credits and public services in the aftermath of the recent economic crisis in the UK are likely to exacerbate the vulnerabilities of workers in non-standard employment.

Of course, workers in standard employment arrangements may be vulnerable as well: heightened economic risk is not the exclusive province of workers in non-standard arrangements. This is particularly true in the UK and the US, whose employment protection frameworks (e.g. dismissal protection) are deemed weak when compared to other industrialised nations.[2]

Nevertheless, non-standard arrangements do have a greater propensity to leave workers vulnerable, as this chapter shows.[3] The US is an important cautionary tale, showing how recent labour market developments – particularly the growth of non-standard employment arrangements – can leave workers vulnerable and deeply exposed to economic risk. Our analysis underlines the importance to such workers of a rights-based approach to employment such as that pursued by UK governments over the last decade. This analysis shows the value of models of welfare provision that are linked to citizenship or residency rights rather than employment status alone – an approach followed by the UK system of social protection. We offer these findings at a time when the future of current employment protection frameworks and inclusive welfare models is being questioned in the UK. We urge policymakers to consider the US experience before pressing ahead with such reforms.

America's distinctive context

When it comes to understanding the living standards of low- and middle-income households, it is necessary to look not only at wages earned and hours worked, but also the extent to which particular types of employment contract induce or protect against economic vulnerability. This is hard to measure: there is no single indicator of job 'precariousness' and employment data do not always make it easy to fully explore the various sources of economic risk.

The link between particular forms of employment – so-called 'non-standard jobs' – and different aspects of vulnerability is significant. The erosion of stable, 'standard' employment arrangements over the past 30 years represents a distinctive shift in labour market structures, which can be traced in the US and the UK as well as other developed countries.

Non-standard jobs entail shorter duration, volatile hours and limited social protections. In the UK, for example, various forms of temporary (non-permanent) employment accounted for 6% of women's and 5% of men's wage employment in 2008.[4] Own-account self-employed (without employees) amounted to 10% of the total UK workforce.[5] In recent years, there have been notable increases in agency workers and temporary public sector workers,[6] and the recession has led to extremely high numbers of people who are working part time involuntarily.[7] Non-standard work may not dominate the UK labour market, but as the US experience shows, the risks these jobs entail for the workers in them are significant.

Visible sources of economic risk or vulnerability from non-standard employment include:

- unpredictable length of employment or expected short duration of employment ('contingency');
- limited or lack of social protections;
- low hourly pay relative to comparable workers in standard employment; and
- low earnings due to low hours and/or irregular work hours.

Some of these characteristics generate liabilities over time as well as in the present. For example, short-term employment usually limits access to firm-provided training and so can entail limited opportunities for career progression.

The increase in employment with such characteristics reflects changes in employer strategies across the developed world, where pressure to increase competitiveness is frequently manifested in the reduction of labour costs. Such strategies have been implemented in environments of declining union power and the deregulation of labour standards.[8] Firms have accessed 'new' labour force entrants, such as women with caring responsibilities, youths and recent immigrants – vulnerable populations who are over-represented in non-standard working arrangements today.

Although these factors have affected the UK as well as the US, there are nevertheless some distinctive characteristics of the US labour market that are key to understanding how non-standard work and economic risk are intertwined:

- US labour markets form a mosaic of settings with divergent norms, regulations and customs. The US is unique among high-income countries in the way its labour markets embody extreme flexibility with few protections. On the one hand, some sectors have formalised personnel policies, with implicitly long-term employment and with 'just cause' dismissal criteria. These are large corporations, sometimes unionised. On the other hand, there are numerous jobs in small- and medium-sized firms with little, if any, codified personnel policy and without collective bargaining coverage. There, the common law standard of 'employment at will' – which presumes that employment may be interrupted at any point by either the employer (most often) or the worker – rules. Furthermore, in pockets, small and scattered work settings – though not necessarily small firms – combine with the heavy use of vulnerable workforces, including undocumented immigrants. There, 'unregulated' employment conditions flourish.[9]

- The US has few universal programmes and places scant legal mandates on employers for labour and social protections. The most important, nearly universal, social protection scheme is the Social Security Act, which provides for minimal old-age pensions, disability insurance and survivor benefits. In principle, it applies to all workers, wage/salary workers and self-employed alike. But there is *no* federally mandated provision of other benefits, such as a supplemental pension plan, health insurance,[10] disability insurance or paid time off for maternity, sickness or holiday. Instead, social protection benefits are provided by employers, often only to their 'standard' workers. This pattern has given rise to a stratified system where workers outside firms with personnel policies and social protection benefits have little social protections.

These distinctive differences make it difficult to compare the US and the UK experience directly. But there are still lessons to learn from US work on economic risk and precarious employment. The US shows how employment protection frameworks and social welfare can mitigate against worker vulnerability – and how their absence can contribute to a more stratified and unequal workforce.

Exploring dimensions of economic vulnerability

Different forms of non-standard employment entail different markers of risk. Here, we draw on our analyses of data from a nationally representative survey (the US Current Population Survey, or CPS), particularly on the most recent year of the Contingent Worker Supplement (2005), to define non-standard employment.[11]

Our analysis shows that three forms of non-standard employment exhibit strong markers of risk: temporary employment; part-time work; and involuntary independent contracting. Temporary employment encompasses explicitly unstable wage employment. Part-time work has a different working-time regime from the standard but also is a distinct arrangement because it comes with little or no employer-based benefits in the US. Independent contractors are self-employed under the tax code and are not subject to core labour and social protections. Involuntary independent contractors are those who would prefer wage employment if available. These categories constitute a subset of non-standard employment. In the next sections, we show here that these types of employment patterns provide lower earnings. We find that they are not distributed equally across the population, mirroring wider social inequalities, and they offer fewer social protections than standard jobs.

Non-standard employment is linked to lower earnings

Working in non-standard jobs has negative implications for worker earnings. Table 2.2.1 summarises the median hourly wage and weekly earnings for workers in temporary employment, part-time employment and independent contracting in the US.

Median *hourly* wages are lower for workers in temporary employment relative to the median for all employed individuals in 2005. Of workers in temporary employment, day labourers reported the lowest median wages (US$8.00/hr) and on-call workers reported the highest (US$10.00/hr). However, median *weekly* earnings among workers in temporary employment were significantly lower than median weekly earnings for the entire employed labour force – often by a factor of 50% or more. Thus, uncertainty in the employment relationship together with lower-than-average hours of work contribute to more pronounced economic risks.

The gender hourly wage/earnings gap – the difference between men's and women's hourly earnings – vanishes within categories of temporary employment, the one exception being on-call workers. However, the gender gap in *weekly* earnings – women's median weekly earnings as a percentage of men's – remains significant. The narrowing of the gender hourly wage gap and the persistence of a gender gap in

Table 2.2.1: Median hourly wages and median weekly earnings by employment type, US, 2005 (US dollars)

	All		Female		Male	
	Wage/hr	Earnings/wk	Wage/hr	Earnings/wk	Wage/hr	Earnings/wk
Short-term hire	$9.00	$300	$9.00	$250	$9.00	$360
Temp agency	$9.50	$388	$10.00	$384	$9.00	$388
Day labourer	$8.00	$240	$8.00	$209	$8.00	$280
On-call	$10.00	$250	$9.50	$197	$11.00	$310
Involuntary part time	$8.00	$212	$8.00	$200	$8.00	$235
Multiple part time	$10.00	$250	$10.00	$250	$8.50	$280
Involuntary independent contractor	$11.00	$480	$10.00	$320	$13.00	$577
All independent contractors	$20.00	$580	$15.00	$352	$20.00	$750
All employed	$11.00	$562	$10.47	$480	$12.00	$673

Source: Labour force statistics from the Current Population Survey (CPS), 2005. Available at: http://www.bls.gov/cps/cpswom2005.pdf

weekly earnings for temporary employment indicate that variability in working-time arrangements remains a source of labour market disadvantage for women in non-standard employment.

Involuntary part-time workers and workers in multiple part-time jobs have the same pattern of earnings as workers in temporary employment: while hourly earnings are somewhat lower, weekly earnings are *significantly below* the median of the total workforce. Hourly gender wage gaps are not evident among involuntary part-time workers and workers with multiple part-time jobs, but women's median *weekly* earnings fall below those of men.

Regarding involuntary contractors, although median *hourly* earnings do not differ markedly from the national averages, median *weekly* earnings are lower than the median for all employed individuals and that for all independent contractors. Average hours of work do not seem to explain the earnings differential. However, the *volatility* of work time, as opposed to its average, is a significant issue: 24% of independent contractors – and 26% of involuntary independent contractors – report having variable work hours as compared to 9.9% of all employed individuals.[12]

There is some evidence that these patterns are mirrored in the UK too. Again, we see that temporary workers[13] have a wider distribution of work hours. Table 2.2.2 shows that temporary workers' median hourly pay is lower than permanent workers but median *weekly* pay is substantially lower, suggesting that shorter hours amplify earnings differences. Within the highest decile of earners, the effect of shorter hours lessens. Conversely, the lowest decile[14] of *weekly* earnings of temporary workers is far lower (half as much) than the lowest decile of weekly earnings of permanent workers. Other research has shown that agency temps experienced an hourly wage penalty of 32% relative

Table 2.2.2: Hourly and weekly earnings by percentile, UK, 2009 (£s)

	Median	10th percentile	90th percentile
Hourly earnings			
Temporary workers	8.84	4.67	21.03
Permanent employees	9.91	5.54	21.26
Weekly earnings			
Temporary workers	230.00	45.00	673.00
Permanent employees	369.00	110.00	819.00

Notes: Figures for the 10th and 90th percentiles refer to the wage levels at those percentiles. Figures are calculated on the basis of the temporary and permanent subsamples of the survey.

Source: Resolution Foundation calculations based on UK Labour Force Survey, April–June 2009

—

to permanent workers in 2007; even taking account of differences in worker characteristics, a 10% wage penalty remains.[15]

Economic vulnerability is not distributed equally

In 2005, there were an estimated 140 million employed individuals in the US (aged 15 and over), 12.7 million of whom worked in one or more of the forms of employment with pronounced economic risks and heightened vulnerabilities along one or more dimensions. Table 2.2.3 shows that these employment categories accounted for 9.1% of all US employment.

Women and minority ethnic groups are disproportionately represented in non-standard employment. The categories featured in Table 2.2.3 account for greater shares of total employment for women than men, African-Americans and Hispanics than whites, and non-citizens than citizens. Involuntary part-time work and multiple part-time jobs account for a larger share of women's total employment compared to the overall population. Among women, higher risks manifest themselves more strongly in terms of non-standard working-time arrangements. The unequal distribution of care work constrains women's time allocation to paid employment and contributes to the

Table 2.2.3: Employment in selected categories of non-standard employment as a percentage of total employment within different population groups, US, 2005 (employed population, aged 15 and over)

			Race/ethnicity				
	All	Female	African-American	Hispanic	White	Other race/ethnicity	Non-citizen
Temporary employment							
Short-term hire	3.3	3.4	3.6	4.7	2.9	4.1	5.9
Temp agency	0.9	1.0	1.9	1.4	0.6	1.0	1.8
On-call	0.9	1.0	1.9	1.4	0.6	1.0	1.8
Day labourer	0.2	0.2	0.2	0.7	0.2	0.1	1.0
All temporary employment	4.5	4.8	5.2	6.4	4.0	5.0	8.0
Part-time employment							
Involuntary part time	2.7	3.3	4.1	4.1	2.2	2.4	4.4
Multi-job part time	1.6	2.2	1.1	0.8	1.8	1.0	0.9
Involuntary independent contractors							
	1.0	0.8	0.7	1.0	1.0	1.3	1.1
All categories	**9.1**	**10.7**	**10.3**	**11.4**	**8.5**	**9.0**	**13.2**

Source: CPS, February 2005.

different incidence of non-standard working-time arrangements among men and women.[16] Similar patterns exist in the UK, with mothers far more likely to work part time than men and with part-time work being concentrated in lower-ranking occupations.[17] Those who work consistently part time are also less likely to enjoy relative upward earnings mobility than those working full time.[18]

A combination of non-standard working-time regimes and unstable employment contributes to higher economic risks for minority racial/ethnic groups, suggesting segregated job opportunities. African-Americans tend to be disproportionately employed by temporary help agencies and in involuntary part-time work. In contrast, Hispanic workers have a noticeably higher probability of working as short-term hires and day labourers, as well as involuntary part-time workers.

The employment categories highlighted here account for a particularly large share of the total employment of non-citizens, revealing a close link between immigration status, economic risk and vulnerability. Importantly, unauthorised immigrants are undercounted in the CPS;[19] the effects on non-citizens and the overall level of non-standard employment are inevitably underestimated as a result.

There is limited access to social protection in non-standard work

Even in the UK, with its much stronger safety nets, there is evidence that temporary workers do worse when it comes to fringe benefits such as holiday entitlements and pensions.[20] However, the picture is much starker in the US, where all these categories of non-standard employment are much less likely to be covered by basic social protections than are workers in 'standard' employment arrangements.

For 2005, approximately 41% of all temporary workers lacked medical insurance, compared to just 14% for individuals in full-time, standard employment arrangements. Only 17% of temporary workers received health insurance from their employers. Coverage is lowest for day labourers, with 61% uninsured, and highest for on-call workers, with 34% uninsured.[21]

Also, in 2005, 61.6% of part-time workers had no access to, or were not eligible for, employer-provided health benefits. Similarly, 71.8% of part-time workers had no access to, or were not eligible for, employer-provided pension benefits.[22]

Being self-employed, independent contractors must cover their own health care and pension benefits. Approximately 40% of involuntary contractors lack medical insurance from any source, compared to 28% of all independent contractors.[23]

Concluding thoughts

We have highlighted the economic risks to which workers in non-standard employment can be exposed in the US context. The economic and financial crisis has made the interactions between labour markets, employment arrangements and economic vulnerability that much more critical. In the UK, fiscal austerity and pressures to roll back social protections as a means to stimulate growth raise serious questions about the relationship between social policies and employment.[24] With reductions in state provision, will pressures mount to provide social benefits through employer-based mechanisms? And will this lead to American-style inequalities? Does the recent growth of part-time employment in the UK signal a permanent change in the distribution of economic risk? Will local government and health services outsourcing, and the abolition of protections of pensions and employment conditions of outsourced workers, create greater numbers of economically vulnerable workers?

The UK is in a stronger position to mitigate the economic risks of non-standard employment, particularly if it reinforces the broad 'rights-based' approach to employment and working conditions pursued over the last decade. Unlike in the US, UK programmes are more universal in scope and basic social protections are not dependent upon working for a particular employer. The UK has begun to implement regulations in keeping with EU directives for non-standard work (fixed term, part time) and, since the end of 2011, these regulations cover agency temp workers too.[25] Importantly, the UK has passed legislation covering workers regardless of status, such as the national minimum wage or paid time off, thus forestalling some discrimination based on work arrangements. This said, similarities between the US and the UK already exist that will need careful monitoring. Hourly and weekly earnings tend to be lower for forms of temporary employment in the UK and temporary workers enjoy fewer benefits compared to individuals in 'permanent' jobs, for example, the right to request flexible working does not extend to temporary workers. Table 2.2.2 showed pronounced differences between the weekly earnings of men and women in low-paid temporary jobs that mirror the patterns in the US. For UK women in non-standard work, low earnings are primarily due to low work hours, not gender wage gaps in hourly pay. Seasonal and casual workers may be classified as self-employed and therefore not subject to labour protections.[27] Nevertheless, opportunities exist that, if seized upon, would help to avert a move towards the stratified system for allocating and managing economic risks of the US.

Finally, in both countries, understanding the full extent and implications of non-standard employment and the changing distribution of economic risk requires comprehensive statistics on the full range of employment arrangements and exposure to risk. Without the ability to assess vulnerabilities arising from changes in the nature of employment, appropriate policy responses will not be forthcoming.

Notes

[1] Carré, F. and Heintz, J. (2009) 'The United States: different sources of precariousness in a mosaic of employment arrangements', in Vosko, L., MacDonald, M. and Campbell, I. (eds) *Gender and the contours of precarious employment*, Oxford: Routledge, pp 43–59.

[2] OECD (Organisation for Economic Co-operation and Development) (2004) 'Employment protection regulation and labour market performance'. Available at: http://www.oecd.org/dataoecd/8/4/34846856.pdf

[3] This chapter is based in part on Carré and Heintz (2009), op cit. For a discussion of precarious employment, see, for example, Vosko, L., MacDonald, M. and Campbell, I. (eds) (2009) *Gender and the contours of precarious employment,* Oxford: Routledge.

[4] Authors' analysis based on Eurostat data. Available at: http://epp.eurostat. ec.europa.eu/portal/page/portal/eurostat/home/

[5] Authors' analysis based on International Labour Office LABORSTA data. Available at: http://laborsta.ilo.org/

[6] Forde, C., Slater, G. and Green, F. (2008) 'Agency working in the U.K.: what do we know?', Policy Report 2, Centre for Employment Relations, Innovation, and Change, University of Leeds, UK.

[7] TUC (Trades Union Congress) (2010) 'Labour market report', July. Available at: http://www.tuc.org.uk/economy/tuc-18224-f0.cfm

[8] Levy, F. and Kochan, T. (2011) 'Addressing the problem of stagnant wages', Employment Policy Research Network. Available at: http://www. employmentpolicy.org/topic/12/research/addressing-problem-stagnant-wages

[9] Bernhardt, A., McGrath, S. and DeFilippis, J. (2007) *Unregulated work in the global city*, New York, NY: Brennan Center for Social Justice.

[10] The US passed a health care reform package in March 2010 – the Affordable Care Act. There is no employer mandate in the legislation but, instead, a set of incentives to encourage employer-provided coverage. Employers with

more than 50 employees would be fined under the Act for not providing health insurance. Small businesses qualify for tax credits if they provide health benefits. Under the existing system, the poor may be eligible for the public health programme Medicaid. Their children may be covered by the State Children Health Insurance Program, whose coverage of poor children varies across states. Finally, the elderly, who may still be active in the labour market, may qualify for the Medicare programme.

[11] Carré and Heintz (2009), op cit.

[12] There is diversity in skill levels across workers and subgroups of workers who are in non-standard arrangements in the US. While skill is not explicitly explored here, the fact that hourly wage differentials between regular and non-standard workers are relatively smaller than weekly earnings differentials suggests that job characteristics (eg hours, stability), rather than individual characteristics such as skill levels, play a role in weekly earnings differentials. Others have also noted that some forms of non-standard work, particularly temporary arrangements, cluster in subsets of occupations and industries. For example, temporary help workers cluster in administrative positions, on the one hand, and production positions in manufacturing, on the other. See Kalleberg, A.L., Reskin, B. and Hudson, K. (2000) 'Bad jobs in America: standard and nonstandard employment relations and job quality in the United States', *American Sociological Review* vol 65, no 2, pp 256–278.

[13] The definition of temporary workers in the UK is taken from the Labour Force Survey (LFS). In the UK LFS, respondents are asked whether their job is permanent or not permanent. In other words, respondents self-define as a temporary worker. The categories for temporary employment in the LFS include those undertaking seasonal work; work done under contract for a fixed period for a fixed task; agency temping; casual work; and work that was temporary in some other way not listed. Seasonal workers are those taken on for jobs that exist only at certain times of the year, for example, fruit pickers or retail staff hired for peak trading seasons such as Christmas. Contract workers are those in employment for a fixed term and can include building contractors and researchers. Agency temps are workers who are paid through an agency for their employment, these are often short-term office jobs such as secretarial or reception work but also include occupations such as chefs.

[14] The lowest decile is the bottom 10% of earners.

[15] Forde et al (2008), op cit.

[16] Allard, M.D. and Janes, M. (2008) 'Time use of working parents: a visual essay', *Monthly Labor Review*, June, pp 3–14.

[17] Neuburger, J., Joshi, H. and Dex, S. (2011) 'Part-time working and pay amongst Millennium Cohort Study mothers', Genet Working Paper 38. Available at: http://www.genet.ac.uk/workpapers/GeNet2010p38.pdf

[18] Savage, L. (2011) *Snakes and ladders*, London: Resolution Foundation.

[19] Passel, J.S., Van Hook, J. and Bean, F.D. (2004) 'Estimates of legal and unauthorized foreign born population for the United States and selected states, based on census 2000: report to the Census Bureau', Urban Institute.

[20] Green, F. (2008) 'Temporary work and insecurity in Britain: a problem solved?', *Social Indicators Research*, vol 88, pp 147–60.

[21] Carré and Heintz (2009), op cit.

[22] Mishel, L., Bernstein, J. and Allegretto, S. (2007) *State of working America 2006/07*, Washington DC: Economic Policy Institute.

[23] Carré and Heintz (2009), op cit.

[24] Grimshaw, D. (2010) 'Labour market policy with a small and shrinking state: the case of the UK', seminar presentation for 'Labour market policy in Europe: Facing the economic crisis', Paris, May.

[25] Until now, they have had an ambiguous employment status.

[26] Green (2008), op cit.

Raising incomes

New evidence and new directions for promoting labour market advancement for low and modest earners

James A. Riccio

A decade ago, concern was growing in the UK and the US about the struggles of low earners to remain steadily employed and move up in the labour market. Evidence on welfare-to-work programmes had shown that many participants who exited such programmes, even successful ones, did not work consistently, and many participants who got jobs earned very low wages, typically joining the ranks of the working poor. In the US, the advent of time-limited welfare made families with only a weak foothold in the labour market especially vulnerable. Yet mainstream employment programmes were not well positioned to address this problem. Typically, they focused on helping non-workers get jobs, rather than offering assistance to help low and modest earners advance. Policy innovators in both countries thus began looking beyond these traditional programmes for ways to help participants who entered work retain employment and move up.

While policymakers recognised the importance of advancement, changes taking hold in the structure of the labour market were making that goal even more challenging. In the US and the UK (and other European countries), labour markets have been polarising since the 1980s. Employment growth and earnings gains were becoming increasingly concentrated among low-skill, low-wage jobs and among higher-skill, higher-wage jobs. Demand for workers to fill middle-skill, middle-wage jobs was lessening.[1] Consequently, the kinds of middle-skill jobs that would represent substantial advancement for people starting in the lower rungs of the labour market, though still a major share of the economy, were becoming relatively more difficult to obtain.

Compounding this challenge was the problem that low-skill, low-wage jobs were not always economically worthwhile for low-income families. Such jobs could result in a loss of cash welfare and related benefits that offset much or most of the gain in earnings, thus discouraging work effort. For some people (especially those with larger families), bigger advancement strides would thus be necessary in order for work to make financial sense. In the US, the expansion of the Earned Income Tax Credit (EITC) in the 1990s and introduction of time-limited welfare and other reforms have increased the economic calculus in favour of work. Britain's more expansive safety net has likely made low-wage work less advantageous than in the US for many low-income families. However, the advent of Universal Credit, which will consolidate benefit programmes and adjust payment rules to help make work pay better than welfare, is intended to increase British benefit recipients' incentive to work. It was against this challenging backdrop that policy innovators in both countries were striving to identify programme strategies that could promote employment retention and advancement among low-income groups. In 1999, the US Department of Health and Human Services launched the Employment Retention and Advancement (ERA) demonstration to build a stronger evidence base in a field almost wholly devoid of reliable evidence on 'what worked'. MDRC, a not-for-profit social policy research organisation headquartered in New York City, was selected as the evaluator. Given the existing knowledge vacuum, the American ERA demonstration cast its net widely and set out to test a variety of approaches, most of which included some forms of 'post-employment' (or 'in-work') guidance and support. In the end, the demonstration included randomised control trials testing 12 different models across six states.

After this project was well under way, transatlantic discussions between MDRC, officials at HM Treasury in the UK and other experts led to the launch of a parallel demonstration project in the UK, also called ERA. Although directly inspired by the US example, the UK demonstration was adapted to a British context.[2] Moreover, it set out to test a single model for different types of people across a variety of places, rather than multiple models.

Both the US and UK ERA studies are now finished. They offer a rich and credible evidence base for understanding what did and did not work when it comes to helping low earners to retain employment and advance in their careers. After commenting briefly on the US study, this chapter summarises the UK findings and goes on to describe a 'next-generation' employment advancement model that is now being tested in the US. That new model draws on a wide range of evidence and builds directly on lessons from the two ERA projects from both sides of the Atlantic in the hope that it will be even more effective than the policy approaches already tested.

Findings from the American Employment Retention and Advancement evaluations

The ERA evaluations in the US underscore the difficult challenge of improving employment retention and advancement among low and modest earners. Of the 12 different retention and advancement models tested, only three succeeded in improving labour market outcomes.[3] One of these programmes (in Riverside, California) served working lone parents who had recently exited the welfare rolls; a second served unemployed lone parents receiving welfare (in two cities in Texas); and a third served lone parents who were working (at low wages) while receiving welfare (in Chicago, Illinois). Each of these programmes, delivered by non-profit or for-profit providers, offered some form of adviser guidance on retention and advancement issues along with other types of assistance.

All three programmes produced increases in participants' earnings over a three- to four-year follow-up period. Most instructive for comparison purposes are the results from the ERA as operated in the city of Corpus Christi, Texas. There, the ERA programme, which offered a combination of financial incentives for sustained full-time employment and post-employment job coaching and guidance, had consistent positive effects on employment retention and earnings, increasing average annual earnings by approximately 15% relative to control group earnings. Moreover, the largest impacts (18%) occurred in the fourth and final year of follow-up. These effects offer evidence that ERA programmes can make a difference for certain groups and are something on which to build.

None of these three effective programmes included a strong emphasis on skills training. At the same time, other US ERA programmes that did offer participants more guidance on and support for skills training did not prove effective. Nonetheless, interest in skills training is growing in the US, particularly in training that is tied more closely to specific occupational sectors. As discussed later in this chapter, the evidence base on the effectiveness of such strategies is thin, but findings from a recent study are encouraging, and new pilots are being planned.

The UK Employment Retention and Advancement Demonstration

Launched in 2003 in selected Jobcentre Plus offices, the UK ERA programme was envisioned as a 'next step' in welfare-to-work policies. Participants in ERA had access to a distinctive set of post-employment job coaching and financial incentives, which were added to the job placement services that unemployed people could normally receive through Jobcentre Plus. These basic features were similar to the core elements of the Texas ERA model mentioned previously. Once employed, ERA participants could receive at least two years of advice and assistance from an employment adviser to help them continue working and advance in work. Those who consistently worked full time could receive substantial cash rewards, called 'retention bonuses'. To support advancement through human capital development, participants could also receive help with tuition costs and cash rewards for completing training courses while employed.[4]

ERA targeted three important groups with different views towards and preparation for work and advancement:

- **'The NDLP group':** unemployed lone parents receiving Income Support and volunteering for the New Deal for Lone Parents welfare-to-work programme.
- **'The WTC group':** lone parents working part time and receiving Working Tax Credit, which supplements the wages of low-paid workers.
- **'The ND25+ group':** long-term unemployed people aged 25 or older receiving Jobseeker's Allowance and required to participate in the New Deal 25 Plus welfare-to-work programme.

These target groups faced different types of challenges that impeded their success in the labour market. A goal of the evaluation was to determine whether ERA could help each of them equally, or whether it worked better for some than others.

The ERA Demonstration was an unusual pilot in the UK because it was being tested *before* government made any commitment to roll it out nationally, and because it adopted a randomised trial approach – a common methodology in the US but used much less often in the UK. In practice, this meant that half of the 16,000 applicants from the six participating regions were randomly assigned to ERA, and the remainder served as a 'business-as-usual' control group. Applicants in the NDLP and ND25+ target groups who became controls continued to receive regular New Deal welfare-to-work services. By randomly dividing the sample into these two groups, the study was able to test conclusively whether or not ERA helped its participants achieve better outcomes than they would have without ERA's help.

Key findings from the UK Employment Retention and Advancement Demonstration[5]

At the time ERA was launched, the New Deal programmes and Jobcentre Plus offered participants little further assistance once they were placed into jobs. Indeed, the lack of a substantive strategy for retention and advancement for low earners was recognised as a major limitation in the New Labour 'workfare' reforms and continues to be an issue today.[6] (Universal Credit is intended to create stronger economic incentives to choose work over welfare, but it will not directly support progression and advancement.) ERA was therefore a major learning opportunity in this field of policy with an otherwise weak evidence base of what actually works. So what did it tell us?

The issue of work and earnings

For each of the two lone-parent groups, ERA caused an early increase in the likelihood of working full time (at least 30 hours per week) rather than part time. This pattern aligns with the programme's requirement that participants work full time in order to qualify for the employment retention bonus. More specifically, for the NDLP group of initially unemployed lone parents, ERA increased the proportion working full time within the first two years after entry into the programme by 10 percentage points, a gain of 34% above the control group's full-time employment rate of 28%. For the WTC group of lone parents already working part time and earning modest wages, ERA increased their likelihood of working full time by 12 percentage points, a gain of 38% above the 30% control group rate.

By leading ERA participants to increase their hours of work, the programme helped them earn more than their control group counterparts – by 9% for the NDLP group and 6% for the WTC group in the first full tax year after random assignment. However, these effects faded in the later years, after the participants left the programme, largely because the control groups caught up.

The earnings gains lasted longer among NDLP lone parents who were better educated (with A-level qualifications), though initially unemployed. This group earned about 16% more than they would have done in the absence of ERA over the four tax years for which earnings data were available. Compared with other unemployed lone parents, this group may have had more unrealised potential to succeed in work, which ERA may have tapped into. From a cost–benefit perspective, workers in this better-educated subgroup were made economically better off *and* the government budget saw a positive return on its investment – which was not the case for the other lone-parent groups.

Of the three main target groups, overall results were most impressive for the ND25+ target group made up of long-term unemployed individuals (mostly men). For them, ERA produced sustained increases in employment and substantial and sustained increases in earnings. Over the four follow-up years, total earnings were about 12% higher for those in ERA compared with those in the control group. These positive effects emerged after the first year and were still evident at the end of the follow-up period. The earnings gains were accompanied by lasting reductions in benefits receipt. Taking into account these and other economic gains and losses (including taxes and programme costs), ERA proved to be cost-beneficial for the participants in this group, and for the government budget. In fact, the Treasury realised a return on its investment of about £4 for every £1 it invested in the programme – a noteworthy achievement for a group that is widely regarded as very difficult to help.

While individual participants may have seen their wages rise during their participation in the programme, the evaluation indicates that ERA did not appear to improve wage rates for any of the three target groups *relative* to their control group counterparts. For example, among the lone-parent groups, workers were earning somewhat more than £8 per hour, on average, by the end of the study. In other words, many of the earnings gains that were observed in the early years of the trial did not come from improved wages, but, rather, from increased hours.

The issue of training

It had been hoped that ERA's incentives and advisory support for taking training courses would help participants build human capital, leading them to earn higher wages. ERA did increase the likelihood of lone parents in the programme participating in training courses. The training effects were especially notable for the WTC group, for whom ERA increased course-taking by almost 13 percentage points (a gain of 22% above the control group average), and increased receipt of training-related qualifications by almost five percentage points (or 16%). The impact on training was positive but smaller for the NDLP group. ERA had no impact on the training rate for the ND25+ group.

Analyses comparing ERA's impacts across target groups and subgroups show that groups for whom ERA increased course-taking did not experience longer-term earnings impacts; conversely, groups that experienced substantial earnings gains (eg the NDLP A-level subgroup and the ND25+ target group) did so without experiencing increases in training. These general patterns suggest that ERA's approach to increasing training did not pay off in the labour market.

Why would this be the case? The problem may have been that those additional participants who took training courses only because of ERA may not have enrolled in training courses that had clear market value for career advancement, or they were not able to find job opportunities in which they could apply their new skills.

Another possible explanation is that ERA may not have provided enough specialised training guidance. ERA advisory staff functioned as employment 'generalists'. They offered general advice and guidance on adapting to work, encouraged participants to consider seeking full-time work, helped them address issues of balancing work and family life, advised them on seeking promotions and finding better jobs, and urged them to enrol in training courses in whatever areas interested them. However, ERA advisers were not expected to have in-depth knowledge of particular occupations or industries or expertise on the career ladders and training requirements for jobs in those areas. Nor were they expected to steer participants assertively towards particular occupations known to offer better advancement opportunities. They were also not positioned to connect participants who had trained in particular occupational areas with relevant employers who were hiring people in those areas.

It is important that the ERA findings are not interpreted to mean that training is irrelevant to advancement. In the UK and the US alike, training and qualifications continue to have a direct and significant association with wages and increases in wage rates, as Larry Mishel and Heidi Shierholz show in Chapter 1.1 of this volume. But the ERA findings do indicate that simply increasing training rates among lower-income groups does not *necessarily* lead to those positive outcomes. Thus, the findings should encourage policymakers to approach the design of future skills-building programmes among low-skilled groups differently, and to test whether their new approaches are effective.

WorkAdvance: a 'next-generation' advancement programme

Both the US and UK ERA demonstrations show conclusively that some post-employment strategies can work for particular groups of low-income adults. They can increase the amount that participants work and how much they earn. They can also leave those participants somewhat better off financially than they would have been in the absence of the programme. In the case of the UK ERA (for the ND25+ group and A-level unemployed lone parents), it also delivered to the government a healthy return on its investment.

This is encouraging evidence. At the same time, it is clear that even the most effective of these strategies achieved their results primarily by inducing participants to work more hours, not by helping them achieve wage rates or salaries higher than they would otherwise have received. So the question remains: is it possible to improve earnings by improving wages and salaries, not simply by increasing the number of hours that low earners work?

This leads back to the question of training. Generally speaking, evidence on the effectiveness of training programmes for low-income groups is limited. Many approaches have not been carefully evaluated, and where stronger evidence exists, the results are mixed. Some studies have shown that many participants start but do not complete training, or obtain credentials that are not well rewarded in the labour market. However, other evidence points to better effects among programmes with strong connections to employers, and among those that increase certain credentials.[7]

As previously mentioned, the UK ERA's positive impact on the receipt of training did not translate into labour market gains, possibly because the programme's approach was too generic and lacked sufficient focus on skills that were in greater demand among employers. One way to do better may be to combine ERA-inspired post-employment assistance with a different approach to skills training, involving more sector-focused strategies. Interest in sector-focused approaches has been growing substantially in the US and the UK alike.[8] Recently, these approaches were given an empirical boost by a small randomised trial completed by the US research organisation Public/Private Ventures (P/PV).[9] This study of three sectoral training programmes found that the programmes increased participants' earnings over two years by 18% (or US$4,500) relative to the control group's earnings. Most of that gain occurred in the second year, after training, when participants' earnings were 29% higher than the control group average.

Important questions remain, of course. For example, can the results from the small P/PV study be replicated across a wider variety of labour markets, population groups and programme providers? Will the effects last longer than two years? Can such programmes, which are much more expensive per person than the various ERA models, be cost-effective? In addition, would adding an ERA-inspired post-employment component (which is rare among sector programmes) enhance their long-term effectiveness?

Hypothesising that combining post-employment services with sector-focused training would be a more powerful intervention than either of those two strategies alone, in 2010, MDRC and partners in the New York City Center for Economic Opportunity[10] set out to design and test a new hybrid model that incorporates both strategies. Called WorkAdvance, this new model will be tested in four cities[11] as a special pilot funded through public and private contributions as an initiative of the federal Social Innovation Fund.[12] The first sites began recruiting sample members in the summer of 2011.

WorkAdvance is intended to help unemployed and low-wage working adults increase their employment and earnings by obtaining good-quality jobs in targeted sectors that have room for advancement through established career pathways. Each of the providers, which are local non-profit organisations, specialises in specific industry sectors in which they have in-depth knowledge and relationships with employers. The providers offer training and advancement services across a range of sectors, including information technology, environmental remediation, manufacturing, health care and transportation.

Participants who are already working must have low incomes and, if they are already employed, be earning no more than US$15 per hour. Like the ERA programmes, WorkAdvance will include a post-employment component, but the non-profit organisations will capitalise on their relationships with employers and help participants understand career opportunities within those or other firms in the same industry. Where appropriate, they will advise on additional training to aid climbing further up a career ladder in a particular sector. For participants for whom the initial job placement turns out not to be a good match (in the view of participants or employers, or both), the advisers will help identify new opportunities.

As with the two ERA projects, this model will be put to a careful real-world test using random assignment. The resulting evidence will show whether it lives up to its promise.

Conclusion

When it comes to helping people progress, low-paid work – on its own – is not necessarily a stepping stone to better jobs. A decade ago, little credible evidence was available to guide US and UK policymakers on what kinds of investments would help low-income individuals improve their standing in the labour market. Much has been learned since then, thanks to serious investments in both countries in rigorously testing new approaches.

This evidence is particularly timely in the UK given the forthcoming introduction of the Universal Credit and the recent implementation of outcomes-based contracts for the Work Programme for welfare recipients. In these reforms, Jobcentre Plus retains an interest in helping low earners achieve steady and better employment. And the private providers, who take on individuals who have the most difficulty in entering employment, have a very strong financial incentive to help those harder-to-help participants not only to find work, but also to remain employed. The findings from the ERA trials in both the UK and US offer relevant lessons. At the same time, it is important to continue to develop and test innovations, including new approaches to skills training, that may be more effective in helping low and moderate earners achieve better economic opportunities.

Notes

[1] Autor, D. (2010) *The polarization of job opportunities in the U.S. labor market: implications for employment and earnings*, Washington, DC: The Center for American Progress and The Hamilton Project of The Brookings Institution. For an alternative assessment suggesting less contraction in middle-skill job opportunities, see Holzer, H. and Lerman, R. (2009) *The future of middle skill jobs*, Washington, DC: The Brookings Institution.

[2] Subsequently, MDRC launched a third demonstration project targeting low-income workers in three cities. Known as the Work Advancement and Support Center (WASC) Demonstration, this initiative combined ERA-like advancement strategies with efforts to help working adults maximise their receipt of government income benefits that they were eligible to receive while employed. The final results for that project will be available in 2012.

[3] See Hendra, R., Dillman, K.-N., Hamilton, G., Lundquist, E., Martinson, K. and Wavelet, M., with Hill, A. and Williams, S. (2010) *The Employment Retention and Advancement project: how effective are different approaches aiming to increase employment retention and advancement? Final impacts for twelve models*. New York, NY: MDRC.

[4] A research consortium carried out the evaluation, which lasted from 2003 through 2011, under a contract with the Department for Work and Pensions (DWP). In Britain, the consortium was headed by MDRC and included the Policy Studies Institute, the Institute for Fiscal Studies, the National Institute of Economic and Social Research and the Office for National Statistics.

[5] For details on the project and final results, see Hendra, R., Riccio, J.A., Dorsett, R., Greenberg, D.H., Knight, G., Phillips, J., Robins, P.K., Vegeris, S.

and Walter, J., with Hill, A., Ray, K. and Smith, J. (2011) *Breaking the low-pay, no-pay cycle: final evidence from the UK Employment Retention and Advancement (ERA) Demonstration*, London: Department for Work and Pensions.

[6] Gregg, P., Harkness, S. and McMillan, L. (2006) *Welfare to work policies and child poverty*, York: Joseph Rowntree Foundation, University of Bristol.

[7] Martinson, K. and Holcomb, P. (2007) *Innovative employment approaches and programs for low-income families*. Washington, DC: The Urban Institute Center on Labor, Human Services and Population.

[8] In the UK, see, for example, the work of the Sector Skills Councils, such as the Women and Work Sector Pathway Initiative. Available at: http://www.ukces.org.uk/ourwork/women-and-work

[9] Maguire, S., Freely, J., Clymer, C., Conway, M. and Schwartz, D. (2011) *Tuning in to local labor markets: findings from the sectoral employment impact study*, New York, NY: Public/Private Ventures.

[10] The Center is a unit within the Office of the Mayor. It oversees the development and testing of innovative anti-poverty initiatives for New York City.

[11] New York City, Cleveland and Youngstown, Ohio, and Tulsa, Oklahoma.

[12] The Social Innovation Fund is a public–private initiative to test the replication and scaling up of evidence-based strategies to help low-income groups. See: http://www.nationalservice.gov/about/programs/innovation.asp

Boosting the pay packets of low- to middle-income families

Daniel P. Gitterman

Over the last decade, the UK's tax credit regime has delivered over £175.4 billion into the purses and wallets of low-earning households. The credits have helped to 'make work pay' for many, and they have supported thousands of people – particularly single mothers – out of poverty and into employment. But the British tax credit regime is not without its critics. There are crucial gaps between policy intent and implementation, which have led to ongoing problems with over- and underpayments. Also, the interactions between the tax credit system and in-work and out-of-work benefits are complex and confusing, leading to some very high marginal tax rates and unusual work incentives, particularly for second earners and larger families.[1]

It is this kind of criticism that is driving the development of the Universal Credit, which will replace the existing system of means-tested benefits and tax credits for working-age adults in the UK beginning in 2013.[2] The Coalition government's ambition to merge in-work support with out-of-work benefits to 'radically simplify the system to make work pay and combat joblessness and poverty'[3] is certainly a bold one. The intuitive appeal of a simplified system is undeniable, as is the policy goal to reduce marginal tax rates and improve work incentives.

However, the US experience suggests that there will always be difficult trade-offs to make between targeted, timely support and simplicity on the one hand, and the generosity of support, work incentives and costs to the Exchequer on the other. This chapter draws on major US studies on the impact of the Earned Income Tax Credit (EITC) on work incentives and wages. It concludes with some reflections on the politics of tax-based assistance at a time when this has become a primary mechanism for redistribution in both the US and the UK.[4]

A brief history of tax credits

Although the American EITC has been in existence since 1975, it was greatly expanded by President Clinton, and now the two largest individual income tax credits – the more targeted, refundable EITC and the more universal Child Tax Credit (CTC) – together represent over US$81.2 billion in tax expenditures in 2011. Given the spending and revenue loss involved, income tax credits have enjoyed an unusually smooth political path: neatly side-stepping limited public support for expanding welfare, at the same time as channelling significant government resources to the pockets of working poor families. From its modest beginnings, the EITC has garnered bipartisan support and widespread popularity over the years. Successive presidents (both Republican and Democrat) refined and improved the EITC, linking it to inflation as part of Reagan's tax reforms of 1986, and finally taking on its current expanded form prior to Clinton's welfare reforms of 1996. Characterised by New Labour's 'hand up, not a hand out' and Clinton's view that 'if you work hard and play by the rules, you shouldn't be poor', both UK and US governments have over time shifted focus – and funding.

Today, more children exit poverty through the EITC than through any other form of government assistance.[5] Figure 2.4.1 shows federal spending on the EITC and the CTC alongside traditional cash assistance benefits. This figure highlights a move away from a cash-based social assistance scheme that constitutes the traditional boundaries of the welfare state, towards tax-based supports designed to lift *working* poor families out of poverty.

This emphasis on work as the route to economic well-being has also driven many of the welfare reforms in the UK. By the end of the 20th century, tax credits had emerged as central elements of a policy regime to boost the pay packets of low-income as well as moderate- and middle-income earners and their children. Income supplements had been around in the UK since 1971, when Conservative Keith Joseph introduced the Family Income Supplement. However, the Working Families Tax Credit introduced by New Labour in 1999 was substantially more generous than any previous measure.

As government transfers via the income tax system have assumed greater significance, two questions arise. First, in an era of widening wage inequalities, what have we learned about the optimal policy design of tax credits? They may be the key mechanism for after-tax income redistribution today, but ongoing problems around targeting, administrative complexity and the sustainability of their costs abound.

Figure 2.4.1: Real federal spending on the EITC, CTC and welfare (AFDC/TANF), FY 1976–2015

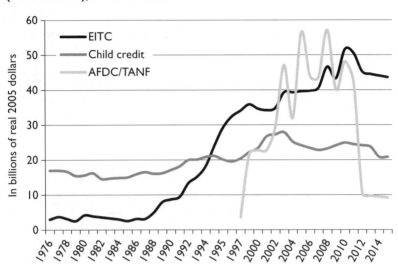

Notes: AFDC – Aid to Families with Dependent Children; TANF – Temporary Assistance to Needy Families; FY – financial year. EITC and CTC aggregate amounts include both outlays and receipts.

Source: FY 2000–06 US Budgets and Internal Revenue Service Statistics on Income data.

This chapter presents some of the US evidence about how the EITC has affected work incentives and wages among low-earning households. This evidence paints a complex picture, and shows how hard it is to make any kind of sweeping statement about the effects and effectiveness of tax credits.

Second, it is clear that government programmes to redistribute post-tax incomes are more important today than they were a generation ago in the household budgets of low earners: UK tax and benefit transfers are doing four times the work that they were in the late 1970s.[6] They account for around one sixth of the total rise in household income among the low- to middle-income group since 1968, despite the fact that their major expansion took place in the past 10 years.[7] But are there limits to what we can expect tax credits to do in the modern labour market? Are current levels of tax credits sustainable given the projected growth of low-paid jobs in Anglo-Saxon economies and the fiscal constraints that shape today's budgetary politics? In the 2012 tax year alone, low- to middle-income households have lost £2.5 billion worth of tax credit support.

Tax credits in the US and UK: key differences in policy design

In contrast to other types of tax expenditures in the US system, tax credits are deducted dollar for dollar directly from taxes owed, rather than reducing the amount of income upon which tax is paid. The result is that a $500 credit is worth the same amount to a family earning $25,000 as to a family on $250,000. Many more individual tax credit dollars today, primarily in the form of the EITC and CTC, go towards low- to moderate-income families than in past decades. These credits have greatly increased the progressivity of the tax and transfer system in the US.

Unlike the UK's tax credits, the EITC and the CTC are both refundable – an important principle that means that the credits can offset regressive payroll taxes, which are often more substantial than income tax for sub-poverty level and minimum wage families in the US. Meanwhile, the effective federal income tax rate is negative for the bottom two quintiles of the income distribution.

The US refund mechanism is also different from that of the UK, with rebates being made annually, based on the previous year's income. All Americans file a tax return, making the additional administrative costs of the tax credit system very low, at less than 1% of the programme costs. This is a notable difference from the UK, where just 15% of people file tax returns – and these are rarely the same people who are eligible for tax credits. So, one of the key benefits for the American regime – its low administrative costs – is less obvious in the UK.

Finally, tax credit payments are calculated based on total family income, in keeping with the joint taxation system of the US. Tax credits are also paid on the basis of household income in the UK, despite Britain's individual-based taxation system.

The impact of tax credits on work incentives

There are two key empirical insights about the effect of the EITC on work incentives that emerge from the US experience: first, there is a notable unevenness across demographic groups in the degree to which the EITC encourages work; and, second, work incentives are driven by the cumulative impact of the total benefits and tax system on a household's income. Together, these insights suggest that policymakers should exercise extreme caution in declaring any particular policy (such as the EITC) unambiguously 'pro–work' or 'anti–work'.

Different incentives for different people

As David Ellwood has argued, all social policies create incentives, and most create at least some that are undesirable. Looking at the EITC, we can see that the incentive effects with respect to labour force participation are overall positive: it encourages some workers to enter the labour force, and it does not induce other individuals, low-skilled or otherwise, to leave it. However, the full empirical story is a little more nuanced than the simple view that the EITC is a straightforwardly pro-work programme.

Previous studies of the EITC have shown that the credit had a particularly positive effect on the labour force participation of single mothers, encouraging them into the workforce in greater numbers than any other group.[8] However, it has had a much more subdued effect on increasing the hours of people already in work. In other words, the impact of tax credits has been far more pronounced when it comes to labour market *participation*, rather than the *intensity* of hours worked.[9]

This can be explained – at least in part – by the design of the EITC. Unlike the UK, US tax credits do not change depending on how many hours are worked; instead, refunds are calculated purely on total household income. The tax credit has a phase-in rate, a flat rate and then a phase-out rate, which begins as soon as a family hits the very low poverty threshold. Table 2.4.1 shows the points on the income distribution that trigger changes in EITC payments. In 2011, 11.8% of EITC payments went to households with adjusted gross incomes under $10,000, 33.5% went to households with incomes between $10,000 and $20,000, 31.3% to households with incomes between $20,000 and $30,0000, and 23.1% was paid to relatively more moderate-income families.[10]

Research shows that the income effect operates to reduce hours worked in the flat region, while income and substitution effects operate to reduce hours worked in the phase-out region. Observational work has also shown that many low earners do not have the option to increase their hours, either due to the nature of their jobs or because of caring responsibilities at home.

These income and substitution effects are particularly pronounced for second earners in two-parent households. Empirical work by Nada Eissa and Hilary Hoynes shows that second earners in households whose incomes place them in the flat to phase-out regions of the EITC should be less likely to work or should work fewer hours.[11] This is due to the fact that – as in the UK – EITC payments in the US are based on total household income, rather than individual wages.

Table 2.4.1: Earned Income Tax Credit parameters, 1975–2011

Calendar year	Credit rate (%)	Minimum income for maximum credit	Maximum credit	Phase-out rate (%)	Phase-out range[a] Beginning income	Ending income
1975–78	10	4,000	400	10	4,000	8,000
1979–84	10	5,000	500	12.5	6,000	10,000
1985–86	11	5,000	550	12.22	6,500	11,000
1987	14	6,080	851	10	6,920	15,432
1988	14	6,240	874	10	9,840	18,576
1989	14	6,500	910	10	10,240	19,340
1990	14	6,810	953	10	10,730	20,264
1991						
One child	16.7	7,140	1,192	11.93	11,250	21,250
Two children	17.3	7,140	1,235	12.36	11,250	21,250
1992						
One child	17.6	7,520	1,324	12.57	11,840	22,370
Two children	18.4	7,520	1,384	13.14	11,840	22,370
1993						
One child	18.5	7,750	1,434	13.21	12,200	23,050
Two children	19.5	7,750	1,511	13.93	12,200	23,050
1994						
No children	7.65	4,000	306	7.65	5,000	9,000
One child	26.3	7,750	2,038	15.98	11,000	23,755
Two children	30	8,425	2,528	17.68	11,000	25,296
1995						
No children	7.65	4,100	314	7.65	5,130	9,230
One child	34	6,160	2,094	15.98	11,290	24,396
Two children	36	8,640	3,110	20.22	11,290	26,673
1996						
No children	7.65	4,220	323	7.65	5,280	9,500
One child	34	6,330	2,152	15.98	11,610	25,078
Two children	40	8,890	3,556	21.06	11,610	28,495
1997						
No children	7.65	4,340	332	7.65	5,430	9,770
One child	34	6,500	2,210	15.98	11,930	25,750
Two children	40	9,140	3,656	21.06	11,930	29,290
1998						
No children	7.65	4,460	341	7.65	5,570	10,030
One child	34	6,680	2,271	15.98	12,260	26,473
Two children	40	9,390	3,756	21.06	12,260	30,095
1999						
No children	7.65	4,530	347	7.65	5,670	10,200
One child	34	6,800	2,312	15.98	12,460	26,928
Two children	40	9,540	3,816	21.06	12,460	30,580

(continued)

Table 2.4.1 (continued)

Calendar year	Credit rate (%)	Minimum income for maximum credit	Maximum credit	Phase-out rate (%)	Phase-out range[a]	
					Beginning income	Ending income
2000						
No children	7.65	4,610	353	7.65	5,770	10,380
One child	34	6,920	2,353	15.98	12,690	27,413
Two children	40	9,720	3,888	21.06	12,690	31,152
2001						
No children	7.65	4,760	364	7.65	5,950	10,710
One child	34	7,140	2,428	15.98	13,090	28,281
Two children	40	10,020	4,008	21.06	13,090	32,121
2002						
No children	7.65	4,910	376	7.65	6,150	11,060
One child	34	7,370	2,506	15.98	13,520	29,201
Two children	40	10,350	4,140	21.06	13,520	33,178
2003						
No children	7.65	4,990	382	7.65	6,240	11,230
One child	34	7,490	2,547	15.98	13,730	29,666
Two children	40	10,510	4,204	21.06	13,730	33,692
2004						
No children	7.65	5,100	390	7.65	6,390	11,490
One child	34	7,660	2,604	15.98	14,040	30,338
Two children	40	10,750	4,300	21.06	14,040	34,458
2005						
No children	7.65	5,220	399	7.65	6,530	11,750
One child	34	7,830	2,662	15.98	14,370	31,030
Two children	40	11,000	4,400	21.06	14,370	35,263
2006						
No children	7.65	5,380	412	7.65	6,740	12,120
One child	34	8,080	2,747	15.98	14,810	32,001
Two children	40	11,340	4,536	21.06	14,810	36,348
2007						
No children	7.65	5,590	428	7.65	7,000	12,590
One child	34	8,390	2,853	15.98	15,390	33,241
Two children	40	11,790	4,716	21.06	15,390	37,783
2008						
No children	7.65	5,720	438	7.65	7,160	12,880
One child	34	8,580	2,917	15.98	15,740	33,995
Two children	40	12,060	4,824	21.06	15,740	38,646
2009						
No children	7.65	5,970	457	7.65	7,470	13,440
One child	34	8,950	3,043	15.98	16,420	35,463
Two children	40	12,570	5,028	21.06	16,420	40,295
Three children	45	12,570	5,657	21.06	16,420	43,279

(continued)

Table 2.4.1 (continued)

Calendar year	Credit rate (%)	Minimum income for maximum credit	Maximum credit	Phase-out rate (%)	Phase-out range[a] Beginning income	Ending income
2010						
No children	7.65	5,980	457	7.65	7,480	13,460
One child	34	8,970	3,050	15.98	16,450	35,535
Two children	40	12,590	5,036	21.06	16,450	40,363
Three children	45	12,590	5,666	21.06	16,450	43,352
2011						
No children	7.65	6,070	464	7.65	7,590	13,660
One child	34	9,100	3,094	15.98	16,690	36,052
Two children	40	12,780	5,112	21.06	16,690	40,964
Three children	45	12,780	5,751	21.06	16,690	43,998

Notes: [a] Beginning in 2002, the values of the beginning and ending points of the phase-out range were increased for married taxpayers filing jointly. The values for these taxpayers were: $1,000 higher than the listed values for 2002–04; $2,000 higher for 2005–07; $3,000 higher in 2008; $5,000 higher in 2009; $5,010 higher in 2010; and $5,080 higher in 2011. Dollar amounts unadjusted for inflation.

Sources: 1975–2003: Joint Committee on Taxation; Ways and Means Committee; and 2004 Green Book. 2004–2009: Internal Revenue Service, Form 1040 Instructions. 2010: Internal Revenue Service, 'Revenue procedure 2009-50' (downloaded 21 October 2009 from: http://www.irs.gov/pub/irs-drop/rp-09-50.pdf). 2011: Internal Revenue Service, 'Revenue procedure 2011-12' (downloaded 13 January 2011 from: http://www.irs.gov/pub/irs-drop/rp-11-12.pdf).

Of course, there are limitations to only economic theory-based thinking in this sphere. It relies on behavioural assumptions that workers fully understand the EITC schedule and are able to calculate how their working patterns throughout the year will determine their tax credits at the end of that year. Unsurprisingly, this has little bearing on real working life.[12] Nevertheless, observational studies confirm the assumptions made by Eissa and Hoynes: while the EITC has substantially driven up the number of single-parent households entering work, it has had a modest negative effect on the labour force participation of secondary earners in two-earner couples in the phase-out region of the EITC. Some studies have suggested that the EITC has no effect even on the *overall* labour supply of married couples, as married men's participation and hours do not appear to be shaped by taxes in the same way that women's are.[13] That said, there has been far less interrogation of the impact of EITC on the labour supply decisions of married couples, and this is an area in need of more research.[14]

Similar second-earner labour supply effects have been documented for married women in the UK. As yet, there have been few workable solutions proposed to addressing these work disincentives in either country's tax credit system. US economists have shown that while moving towards an individual-based (rather than joint) EITC would deliver on the main policy objective (to support work), it would also be prohibitively expensive – adding an estimated US$11 billion to each year's bill. Furthermore, such a move would have distributional consequences: the EITC would move from supporting low–income families specifically, to supporting *all* low-earners – many of whom live in much richer households further up the income distribution.

Integration with other benefits and supports

Advocates of the EITC argue that redistribution occurs with much less distortion to labour supply than that caused by other elements of the cash-assistance-based welfare system. Critics, however, point to the marginal tax rates in the phase-out rate of the credit – which can be very high when the EITC is combined with federal, state and payroll taxes.

A comparison of the US and the UK is instructive here. Work incentives appear to be stronger in the US.[15] There are two main explanations for this. First, the interaction of work-based credits with the tax and benefit system in the UK has the effect of dampening work incentives. Unlike the US system, in the UK, income from in-work benefits is counted as income in the calculation of other benefits – in particular, housing benefits.

Second, much of the increase in the generosity of in-work benefits has been matched in the UK by increases in the generosity of the income transfers available to out-of-work families with children underpinned by universal benefits such as child benefit (which has been recently reformed and means-tested). In particular, low-income out-of-work families benefited from increases in child tax credits (in the early 2000s) as did families in work. Furthermore, investment in a free universal childcare offer has boosted the living standards of all low- to middle-income families through in-kind support for employment and child development. The US picture offers a significant contrast: there has been a relative decline in the value of out-of-work income supports.

The contrasts between the US and the UK illustrate an important point: by definition, work incentives demand a clear differentiation between what support a worker gets when unemployed and what support they would get if they were in work. Increasing in-work benefits in order to make this differentiation entails an economic cost for the Exchequer. On the other hand, as we have seen in the US, reducing out-of-work benefits is likely to generate significant increases in poverty rates, especially during economic downturns. Is it fair to punish workers and their families with cripplingly low out-of-work supports and time-limited benefits when there are simply not enough jobs to go round for unemployed and actively searching workers?

So the US experience should be a reminder to UK policymakers that tax and welfare systems have multiple goals. Work incentives are, of course, centrally important. But so too is the need to ensure that families are not left in abject poverty if they are unable to find work. As a result of cuts to tax credits in the UK, projections show significant increases in child poverty over the next 10 years, reversing the gains made since 1999 by the end of the decade.[16]

The need for caution

Taken together, these findings suggest that reformers should exercise caution in declaring any particular policy unambiguously 'pro-work' or 'anti-work'. Traditional means-tested benefits usually create clear and systematic work disincentives and marriage penalties. In contrast, tax credits create sharply different incentives for different individuals, depending on their level of earnings and marital situation.[17] The effects on work incentives are hard to predict by economic assumptions alone. Furthermore, work incentives depend in part on what benefits are available in the absence of work, and in part on how tax credits interact with other benefits and work supports.

For the last decade, some of the finest minds in the UK and the US have tried to come up with a tax credit and benefit system that 'makes work pay' for everyone. The fact that this remains an elusive goal in both countries suggests that the UK government should be careful not to over-claim the likely impacts of the Universal Credit. While simplification is an important and legitimate goal, the risk is that it might produce a system with new challenges and distortions of its own. Early analysis shows that the Universal Credit is unlikely to significantly improve marginal tax rates, with work incentives being worse for second earners who want to increase their hours beyond part time.[18]

Tax credits versus low wages: compliments or substitutes?

In *Boosting paychecks: the politics of supporting America's working poor*, Gitterman argues that income tax credits and the federal minimum wage emerged as the two central strategies used by governments in the latter part of the 20th century to boost the pre-tax earnings and post-tax incomes of low-earning households.[19] Gitterman noted that in political terms, tax credits had been much more successful than the minimum wage in terms of garnering bipartisan support. Others have argued that tax credits have advantages in terms of outcomes too.[20] Because of the income restrictions of the EITC, it is a more targeted policy intervention in low-wage labour markets. The evidence of policy interactions between the EITC and the minimum wage also indicates that research on the distributional effects of only one policy in isolation may be too narrow.

Andrew Leigh has used variations in state-level EITCs to explore the impact of EITC on wage levels. He finds that the net effect of increasing the generosity of the EITC is to *reduce* hourly wages for low-skilled workers. A 10% rise in the generosity of the credit reduces hourly wages for high school dropouts by 5%, and reduces wages for those with only a high school diploma by 2%. The EITC has no effect on the wages of college graduates. Although the EITC has a much larger effect on the labour force participation of workers with children than those without, the *wage* effect appears to be similar for workers with and without children. This suggests that when it comes to wages, what matters is the average EITC rate in a labour market, not an employee's own EITC rate.[21]

In this light, economists such as Richard Freeman argue that the redistributive effects of a minimum wage depend on the labour market and redistributive system in which it operates, on the level of the minimum, and on its enforcement. At best, an effective minimum wage will shift the earnings distribution in favour of the low paid and buttress the bottom tiers of the distribution from erosion. At worst – and the evidence is inconclusive here – minimum wages reduce the share of earnings going to the low paid by displacing many workers from employment altogether. In Freeman's view, neither outcome is certain, and so embracing a minimum wage is a risky but potentially beneficial move.

Since Freeman made his case for the minimum wage as a redistributive tool in 1996, studies in the US have shown that increases in the minimum wage are not only good for low earners, but also have no adverse effects on businesses or the wider economy.[22] Indeed, some economists have shown how the wage offers substantial benefits in the form of higher productivity, decreased turnover, lower recruiting and training costs, decreased absenteeism, and increased worker morale.[23] Moreover, if a US and UK minimum wage directs the attention towards the need to develop long-term policies that augment the productivity and skills of the low paid, and of the firms for whom they work, it can provide an additional service as well as redistributing modest amounts to the low paid.[24]

In this context, some US reformers look to the UK's national minimum wage with great envy. Despite the many battles fought to expand the coverage of the US minimum wage and to raise its hourly compensation, the wage does only a little to 'make work pay'. Never indexed, the minimum wage's value eroded by 30% over the 1980s in the US as Congress failed to uprate it for nine consecutive years. In 2010, it was worth less in real terms than it was in 1955. Today, a person working full time and year-round on the minimum wage would bring home $15,000 a year – $6,000 below the already-low poverty threshold for a family of four. Recent studies have shown widespread violations of wage and hours laws – with one estimating that such violations effectively lower the wages of affected workers by 15%.[25] While the national minimum wage in the UK has fared better, the picture is not altogether rosy. The national minimum wage has failed to keep up with inflation in recent years, with the 2011 cash increase representing the single biggest fall in the value of the minimum wage. Furthermore, no more than 5% of adult workers are paid the minimum wage in the UK, leaving a large low-wage labour market intact.[26]

In today's straitened economic circumstances, it is likely that both US and UK governments will need to focus on boosting pay packets through improved pre-tax earnings, as well as continuing to redistribute post-tax income via the tax credit system and benefits. It is vital that the UK protects and extends its minimum wage legislation in the years to come, as well as thinking about how to improve the design of tax credits.

Conclusion: the politics of boosting pay packets

This chapter has focused on the behavioural effects and policy outcomes of tax credits. But many US political scientists add a further consideration – the extent to which a particular policy design builds or undermines broad-based political support for government redistribution programmes. When it comes to tax credits, the research offers mixed findings.

The prevailing wisdom among many US-based political scientists suggests that narrowly targeted income transfers, such as direct cash assistance to low-income families, enjoy only sporadic political support, as they tend to be enacted in periods of partisan imbalance and to be vulnerable to retrenchment when elections shift the balance of power. The EITC, as a targeted individual credit with employment incentives and distributional impacts, is a notable counter-example to the conventional wisdom. Robert Greenstein, Director of the Center for Budget and Policy Priorities, believes that the eligibility of moderate-income households alongside poor families is therefore what strengthened the underlying political support for EITC, commenting that 'if the public considers benefits to be earned, or strongly approves of the services being provided, political strength can be sustained among targeted means-tested programs'.[27]

These findings are echoed by research elsewhere. For example, an international study from 1998 identified a 'paradox of redistribution' – showing that countries that target more tightly have less success in reducing poverty or in building a groundswell of support for this as a legitimate objective.[27] In light of this, UK reformers should push for a 'targeted within universal' credit and pay careful attention to the proposed Universal Credit parameters. According to proponents of this approach, it can reinforce political support for assistance to low-income working families by linking it to a credit that also benefits moderate- and middle-income families.

However, there is also evidence that providing income support through the income tax code *undermines* the links people make between certain benefits and government action. For example, 47% of Americans benefiting from EITC and 52% of people receiving the Child Tax Credit do not believe they have received support from the federal government.[28] If the figures are similar in the UK, this may well explain why the price paid by the Coalition (so far) for the major reductions they have made to tax credits is not as high as some predicted.

So, designing an income tax credit is as much a political choice as an exercise in policy analysis. But as UK political parties debate the optimal design of the Universal Credit, they need to remember that while tax credits may help to mitigate against stagnating wages and rising living costs, they do not prevent them in the first place. In this context, it is hard to see how governments can seriously advance a political and policy agenda for boosting pre-tax pay packets without focusing more than they have done in the recent past on re-establishing the links between pay and productivity. The greatest challenge for 21st-century politicians on both sides of the Atlantic is finding a more sustainable and equitable way of balancing the flexibility of the labour market with economic security for low- to middle-class households.

Notes

[1] Economic Dependency Working Group (2009) 'Dynamic benefits: towards welfare that works', Centre for Social Justice. Available at:

http://www.centreforsocialjustice.org.uk/client/downloads/csj%20
dynamic%20benefits%20exec%20web%20new.pdf

[2] Brewer, M., Browne, J. and Jin, W. (2011) 'Universal Credit: a preliminary analysis', Institute for Fiscal Studies Available at: http://www.ifs.org.uk/publications/5415

[3] Department for Work and Pensions (2010) *Universal Credit: Welfare that works*, London: The Stationery Office.

[4] HM Revenue and Customs (2011) *Annual report and resources accounts 2010-11*, London: TSO. Available at: http://www.hmrc.gov.uk/about/annual-report-accounts-1011.pdf; Office of Management and Budget (2010) 'Budget of the United States Government, FY 2011, analytical perspectives, tax expenditures section', pp 212–13. Available at: http://www.taxpolicycenter.org/numbers/displayatab.cfm?DocID=3138&topic2ID=60&topic3ID=65&DocTypeID=1

[5] Greenstein, R. (2005) *The earned income tax credit: boosting employment, aiding the working poor*, Washington, DC: Center for Budget and Policy Priorities; Greenstein, R. and Shapiro, I. (1998) *New research findings on the effects of the earned income tax credit*, Working Paper No 98-022, Washington, DC: Center on Budget and Policy Priorities, available at: http://www.huduser.org/portal/publications/ReductionofWCHNAssistedHousing.pdf, quoted in National Poverty Center Working Paper Series (2010) *The role of Earned Income Tax Credit in the budgets of low-income families*, June, Ann Arbor, MI: University of Michigan.

[6] Plunkett, J. (2011) *Growth without gain? The faltering living standards of people on low-to-middle incomes*, London: Resolution Foundation, Figure 24.

[7] Brewer, M. and Wren-Lewis, L. (2011) *Why did Britain's households get richer? Decomposing UK household income growth between 1968 and 2008–09 (IFS analysis for the Resolution Foundation)*, London: Resolution Foundation.

[8] Eissa, N. and Liebman, J.B. (1996) 'Labor supply response to the Earned Income Tax Credit', *Quarterly Journal of Economics*, vol 111, no 2, pp 606–37.

[9] Eissa, N. and Hoynes, H.W. (2004) 'Taxes and the labor market participation of married couples: the Earned Income Tax Credit', *Journal of Public Economics*, vol 88, nos 9/10, pp 1931–58.

[10] Office of Management and Budget (2010), op cit, pp 212–13.

[11] Eissa, N. and Hoynes, H.W. (2004), op cit.

[12] Hotz, V.J. and Scholz, J.K. (2003) 'The Earned Income Tax Credit', in R. Moffitt (ed) *Means-tested transfer programs in the United States*, Chicago, IL: The University of Chicago Press and NBER.

[13] Eissa, N. and Hoynes, H. (2004), op cit.

[14] Hotz, V.J. and Scholz, K.J. (2003), op cit.

[15] Blundell, R. and Hoynes, H.W. (2004) 'Has "in-work" benefit reform helped the labor market?', in D. Card, R. Blundell and R.B. Freeman (eds) *Seeking a premier economy: the economic effects of British economic reforms, 1980–2000*, Chicago, IL: University of Chicago Press.

[16] Brewer, M., Browne, J. and Joyce, R. (2011) *Child and working age poverty from 2010 to 2020*, London: Institute for Fiscal Studies.

[17] Ellwood, D.T. (2001) 'The impact of the Earned Income Tax Credit and social policy reforms on work, marriage, and living arrangements', in B. Meyer and D. Holtz-Eakin (eds) *Making work pay: the Earned Income Tax Credit and its impact on America's families*, New York, NY: Russell Sage Foundation.

[18] Hirsch, D. (2011) *Childcare and the hours trap*, London: The Resolution Foundation.

[19] Gitterman, D.P. (2010) *Boosting paychecks: the politics of supporting America's working poor*, Washington, DC: Brookings Institution Press.

[20] Hotz, V.J. and Scholz, J.K. (2000) 'Not perfect, but still pretty good: the EITC and other policies to support the US low wage labour market', *OECD Economics Studies No. 31*. Available at: http://www.oecd.org/dataoecd/23/6/2697856.pdf

[21] Leigh, A. (2010) 'Who benefits from the Earned Income Tax Credit? Incidence among recipients, co-workers and firms', *The B.E. Journal of Economic Analysis and Policy*, vol 10, no 1. Available at: http://people.anu.edu.au/andrew.leigh/pdf/EITC%20incidence.pdf

[22] Card, D. and Krueger, A. (1995) *Myth and measurement: the new economics of the minimum wage*, Princeton, NJ: Princeton University Press.

[23] Fox, L. (2006) 'Minimum wage trends: understanding past and contemporary research', Economic Policy Institute Briefing Paper #178, November. Available at: http://epi.3cdn.net/69f6625aa0868c59ab_1rm6bnk93.pdf

[24] Freeman, R. (1996) 'The minimum wage as a redistributive tool', *The Economic Journal*, vol 106, no 436, pp 639–49.

[25] Levy, F. and Kochan, T. (2011) 'Addressing the problem of stagnant wages', Employment Policy Research Network. Available at: http://www.employmentpolicy.org/topic/12/research/addressing-problem-stagnant-wages

[26] Manning, A. (2012) *Minimum wage: maximum impact*, London: The Resolution Foundation.

[27] Greenstein, R. (1996) 'Universal and targeted approaches to relieving poverty: an alternative view', in C. Jencks and P. Peterson (eds) *The urban underclass*, Washington, DC: Brookings Institution Press.

[28] Korpi, W. and Palme, J. (1998) 'The paradox of redistribution and strategies of equality: welfare state institutions, inequality and poverty in Western countries', *American Sociological Review*, vol 63, no 5, pp 661-687.

[29] Mettler, S. (2010) 'Reconstituting the submerged state: the challenge of social policy reform in the Obama era', *Perspectives on Politics*, September, p 809.

Strengthening economic security

Strategies to expand the affordable private rental stock

Keith Wardrip[1]

Like the UK, the US is a nation of homeowners. Although millions have lost their homes to foreclosure in recent years, 81% of Americans still believe that buying a home is the best long-term investment one can make, down only very slightly compared to 1991.[2] Home ownership is supported by a policy environment that has encouraged it via a range of fiscal initiatives, and a mortgage market that – until recently – made it easy for most qualified households to obtain a loan.

But for many in today's economy, home ownership is out of reach. While the vast majority of the US's 39 million renter households would like to become homeowners, three quarters cannot afford to make this transition.[3] Unemployment and underemployment have suppressed household incomes, and although lower than during the bubble, home prices are still not affordable for many working families. The rented sector will therefore continue to play a significant role in housing Americans, particularly low- and modest-earning Americans, in years to come. The same is true in the UK. It would take the average low- to middle-income household in the UK 21 years to accumulate a deposit to buy the average first-time buyer home, assuming that they save 5% of their income each year.[4]

In the US, as in the UK, roughly one third of all households live in a rented home, but there are considerable differences in the share that live in subsidised housing. The UK currently takes a much more direct approach to achieving the goal of affordable housing for low- and modest-income families, directly subsidising housing in two main ways: either by the state providing accommodation through social housing, or through subsidising private sector rents via the benefits system in the form of a means-tested Housing Benefit. In total, roughly 17% of all households in England live in social rented housing.[5] In contrast, only about 7 million of the 39 million renter households in the US – or 6% of all households – live in federally assisted housing,[6] a number that falls not only well below England's experience, but also far short of demand given that more than 9 million renters nonetheless spend more than half of their income on housing.[7]

There are indications that affordability issues may become even more acute in the future, as a shortage of debt financing in recent years has slowed the construction of rental housing in the US. Analysts expect only 53,000 multi-family apartments to be completed in 2011,[8] compared to an annual average of 230,000 between 1996 and 2009.[9] Household formation delayed by the recession is expected to pick up when the economy improves, which is likely to increase demand for new rental units to well over 150,000. The result is likely to be a falling vacancy rate and, inevitably, a tighter and higher-priced rental sector.[10]

These issues are not unique to the US. Resolution Foundation analysis shows that this affordability crisis is mirrored in the UK and will only worsen in the years to come as housing supply fails to keep up with demand. Supply constraints due to poor access to development and mortgage finance are compounded by a series of policy changes that are reshaping the housing market. The numbers of low- to middle-income households in social housing is unlikely to grow given significant cuts to the capital grant available for the expansion of social housing. Government investment in the sector is set to fall during the current Spending Review period from £6.8 billion in 2010/11 to £2 billion in 2014/15, a cut of 74%. Furthermore, it is unclear whether social housing will continue to meet the needs of vulnerable households as rents can now be charged at up to 80% of local market rents rather than the previous ceiling of 60%. At the same time, the government has lowered the cap on Housing Benefit changes, which will push many low-income families into the lowest-quality reaches of the private rented sector and will force some out of major cities. So how should governments respond to the challenge of providing for affordable rented accommodation in a world where direct provision of housing or rent support is, at best, a small part of the solution?

In a booming economy, local governments on both sides of the Atlantic capitalised on market-rate developments by requiring developers to make a specified share of planned housing units affordable to low- and moderate-income households. Referred to as 'inclusionary zoning' in the US and as 'Section 106' (from section 106 of the Town and Country Planning Act 1990) in the UK context, this strategy can be hugely successful where housing demand and development are strong. However, since the economy crashed, many Section 106 agreements have faltered. In the UK, local councils are still struggling to re-engage developers in delivering affordable homes as part of their market-rate plans.

It remains to be seen whether this model will recover in the UK as the economy improves. Whatever happens, it is clear that leveraging more private investment to deliver affordable rented accommodation is likely to be a central part of any approach in the future given the fiscal crisis gripping us today. As a consequence, the UK government has commissioned an independent review into the possibilities of attracting private investment from large financial institutions such as pension funds into the UK rented sector. The historic emphasis on market-shaping in the US has yielded some valuable insights about what national, state and local governments can do to attract more institutional investment into the private rented sector, above and beyond the Section 106 approach, which can inform developments in the UK. This chapter critically examines several policy approaches that are currently in use in the US to stimulate a more affordable rental market.[11]

Low Income Housing Tax Credits

The Low Income Housing Tax Credit (LIHTC) programme was designed to encourage private investment in affordable housing. Since passage of the Tax Reform Act in 1986, the federal government has given states the authority to issue federal tax credits to encourage the development of affordable rental housing. State housing finance agencies allocate their tax credits to developers on a competitive basis, which allows them to select projects that best meet the criteria spelled out in the state's qualified allocation plan (QAP).[12] Investors purchase the credits, either directly from the developer or from a broker, thereby providing equity for the rental development.[13] In 2011, a state's authority to allocate tax credits was capped at US$2.15 per person (eg US$21.5 million for a state with a population of 10 million), with a minimum of US$2.5 million awarded to the smallest states.[14]

Investors in the credits provide much of the up-front equity to construct or substantially rehabilitate an affordable property – either 70% or 30% of the costs associated with the affordable units, depending on the type of credit. In return, the investor can claim an amount equal to the investment as a credit against federal taxes (allocated over a 10-year period). In addition to the tax credit, the depreciation of the property and interest expenses further lower an investor's taxable income, and these features combine to create an attractive return on investment.[15] Typically, LIHTC investors focus on tax benefits rather than on cash flow (which is usually minimal) or on residual real estate value (which is highly uncertain at the time of the investment) when evaluating opportunities. By 1994, institutional investors – primarily large banks and the government-sponsored enterprises Fannie Mae and Freddie Mac – had replaced individual investors as the dominant financial participants in the programme, and, by 2002, they constituted 95% of the equity contribution.[16] This supports evidence from other countries such as Germany and Switzerland that a supportive tax regime can be critical in stimulating institutional investment.[17]

Rental properties funded through the LIHTC programme are required to make a certain percentage of their units affordable to low-income households: either 40% of the units need to be affordable at 60% of the area median income, or 20% need to be affordable at 50% of the area median. Rent-restricted units are typically required to remain affordable for at least 30 years, and states must give priority to projects with longer affordability periods. On the other hand, under certain circumstances, it is possible for the period of affordability to end after 15 years.

The success of the LIHTC programme can be measured in its production levels. Roughly 1.9 million rental units have been constructed or substantially rehabilitated under the programme since its inception, and annual levels exceeded 125,000 between 2003 and 2005. Annual production is estimated to have fallen to 75,000 units in the wake of the housing crisis,[18] reflecting the drop-off in housing construction generally. But in addition to falling victim to weakening housing demand, the demand for tax credits in particular waned because fewer corporate investors were reporting profits and thus had scant need for the tax shelter that the programme provides. Despite the generally sluggish US economy and the withdrawal of Fannie Mae and Freddie Mac from the pool of potential investors, there is evidence that interest from other corporate investors has returned and the value of the tax credit has rebounded. Some even believe that when 2011 draws to a close, the volume of the tax credit market could approach pre-recession levels.[19]

One criticism of the programme is that it functions only during periods of healthy corporate profits. Another is that without other forms of rental assistance, LIHTC rents are generally not affordable to households earning less than 50% or 60% of the median income. The need to layer deeper subsidies onto an LIHTC property in order to serve the poorest households can complicate the development process and calls into question the efficiency of the programme for serving households with the lowest incomes. These criticisms aside, the LIHTC programme effectively serves the households for which it is targeted and is the single-largest affordable housing production programme in the US.

Real Estate Investment Trusts

There has been considerable UK interest in the Real Estate Investment Trust (REIT) model that is a familiar part of the US rental market. A REIT is a real estate company that typically specialises in a specific type of property: office parks, shopping malls or, of particular interest here, rental properties. Using investor capital, an apartment REIT assembles and manages a portfolio of properties and redistributes rental income to its investors. Tax law in the US exempts REITs from corporate income tax as long as 90% of all profits are paid as dividends.[20] In addition to being the housing provider for thousands of households, an apartment REIT allows investors lacking the capital to directly buy commercial property to nevertheless have a financial stake in the sector. In total, 10 REITs rank among the 50 largest apartment owners and, collectively, REITs own 3.4% of the US multi-family rental market.[21]

There is no direct connection between the typical REIT and the supply of affordable rental homes in the US. In fact, because REITs are beholden to their investors, their objective is to maximise the income that their portfolio produces. But indirectly, by providing an avenue for investor participation in the multi-family residential market, REITs can increase the demand for the asset and thus influence supply. A greater supply of multi-family rental properties – even those with higher rents – can create downward pressure on the rents of existing properties.

Although the typical REIT plays no direct role in the affordable housing sector, REITs can be created to advance social objectives. Just as a 'socially responsible' mutual fund might invest only in 'green' companies or those that avoid product-testing on animals, for example, a mission-driven REIT can choose to acquire and manage only affordable housing properties. Admittedly an exception to the rule, a REIT that specialises in affordable housing can play an important role in acquiring and rehabilitating threatened projects that might otherwise be removed from the affordable housing stock.[22] With this possibility in mind, the UK government is consulting on the viability of social housing REITs to increase investment in affordable rented homes, replacing traditional grant funding from government.

Some have argued that the presence of such large-scale investors in the US is a distinctive feature of the housing market structure there, with its 'deep' urban markets containing high proportions of renters living in large blocks. Such markets minimise investment risks and enable economies of scale – two essential factors for encouraging REIT involvement. Table 2.5.1 shows the extent to which institutional

Table 2.5.1: The relationship between institutional investment and the scale of developments in the United States

	Distribution of rental units by property size	Per cent of properties owned by individuals
1 unit	37%	83%
2–4 units	19%	85%
5–49 units	33%	61%
50+ units	11%	13%

Source: Tabulations of the 2009 American Community Survey Public-Use Microdata Sample housing file and *Residential Finance Survey: 2001*, published in September 2005 by the US Census Bureau and the US Department of Housing and Urban Development.

investment is linked to scale, playing a much more significant role in the market for large apartment block rentals than for smaller properties.

The UK's fragmented market, where three quarters of landlords are individuals or couples owning one or two units, has less obvious appeal for REITs to buy in bulk and manage at acceptable economies of scale. However, Jones suggests that the increasingly blurred boundaries between the private and social housing sectors in the UK offer potential for the growth of the REIT model.[23] He sees the large-scale purchase of existing housing stock, or the conversion of existing housing associations to REITs, as a policy opportunity yet to be fully realised.

The Low-Income Housing Tax Credit programme and REITs both facilitate the flow of investor capital into the private rental sector, and both depend on the federal tax code for their existence. They are inherently national in scope, although the LIHTC programme is certainly shaped by state and local actors. The following section shifts the scale to the local government level and explores tax increment financing as a mechanism to increase the supply of rental housing that low- and moderate-income households can afford.

Tax increment financing

While new to the UK, municipal governments in the US have been able to borrow against predicted economic growth in their area for some time. Many localities make use of this power to actively stimulate local growth through 'tax increment financing' (TIF). Through this process, the local government makes funds available, often by issuing bonds to investors, for infrastructure improvements or investments in other public amenities in anticipation of attracting additional private sector interest and increasing land values in the TIF district. The successful implementation of this strategy results in incremental property tax revenue, which is used to repay the initial investment.

While there is not a federal requirement to do so, local communities committed to expanding affordable housing through TIF can take one of several approaches. The safest – and perhaps most effective – approach may well be to require a share of the tax increment generated through the improvements to be used to fund the construction of affordable rental and for-sale homes. Without such a commitment, there is a real risk that rising land values in the TIF district will not only preclude the development of new affordable housing, but also raise the appeal, and therefore the rents, of existing housing in the area.

In California, enabling legislation requires 20% of all TIF funds to be invested in the construction or preservation of affordable housing. This share can amount to over US$1 billion annually, and nearly 100,000 homes for low- and moderate-income households have been supported state-wide by the work of redevelopment agencies.[24] Likewise, 20% of TIF proceeds in Utah must be used to build or preserve affordable housing in any TIF district generating more than US$100,000 in annual revenue.

A more direct but less common approach is to use TIF explicitly to develop affordable housing. One example is the Affordable Housing Tax Increment Financing programme, operated by the Maine State Housing Authority. Under this programme, a municipality defines a TIF district and creates a plan for increasing the supply of affordable housing therein. If approved by the state, the municipality can use the incremental property tax revenue generated by the new affordable housing units to help fund project development costs, offset ongoing operating costs or cover community costs associated with the new housing, such as infrastructure or education. This programme has supported at least 20 projects since its inception in 2004.[25]

Traditional TIF is not without its critics. One criticism is that the process simply redistributes growth and does not affect aggregate property values in a municipality; where this is the case, no city-wide tax increment is actually created to repay the initial investment.[26] Another claim is that TIF siphons off property tax revenue increases that would have occurred in the absence of the TIF-related investment. These are concerns that cities should consider before embarking on TIF as an economic development tool. For those that do, however, any strategy that effectively increases property values in a targeted area should include measures – such as the mandatory set-aside used in California and Utah – to ensure that low- and moderate-income households are not displaced from revitalising areas.

Accelerated Development Zones, which were introduced in the UK in 2010, are beginning to incorporate TIF and other similar approaches, enabling local authorities to borrow against predicted growth in business rates. The concept has enjoyed cross-party support and has featured frequently in the Coalition's strategies for regeneration and local growth. The US experience underlines the importance of ensuring that any strategy designed to increase property values in a targeted area includes specific measures to prevent displacement and ensure that new residential developments are designed to be socio-economically inclusive, as suggested here.

Conclusions

In the US, successful efforts to expand affordable rental housing options for low- and moderate-income households depend on effective housing programmes, creative financing mechanisms and opportunities for institutional investment. While federal policies play a crucial role in this process, it remains the case that local governments play an equally important role: in identifying a failure of the housing market to provide ample affordable options; in developing a housing plan to address the failure; in building public support for the plan; and in enacting the appropriate policies and programmes to put the plan in motion.

Public support is not a given, however, and the best laid plans can come to naught without sufficient political will. Many elected officials and their constituents alike voice concerns about the impact of affordable rental housing on traffic congestion, schools, property values, crime and the tax base. Without proper encouragement, some municipalities exercise their land-use authority to the detriment of the housing needs of their lower-income citizens. Where this is the case, federal and state governments can and should require or incentivise local governments to provide their 'fair share' of affordable housing.

There is no single way to develop private, low-cost rental housing in the US, and while never an easy task, today's constrained fiscal environment makes it that much more difficult. Federal, state and local governments continue to experiment with new strategies to expand housing choices for low- and moderate-income households without imposing an undue burden on any of the public or private actors involved. Learning from this continued experimentation, and sharing the results with others facing the same challenges, is key to addressing the shortage of affordable housing in communities across both countries.

Notes

[1] Special thanks to Ethan Handelman at the National Housing Conference and Rebecca Cohen at the Center for Housing Policy for their thoughtful reviews and suggestions.

[2] Pew Social Trends Staff (2011) *Home sweet home. Still: five years after the bubble burst*, April, Washington, DC: Pew Research Center. Available at: http://pewsocialtrends.org/2011/04/12/home-sweet-home-still/

[3] Ibid.

[4] Whittaker, M. (2012) *Essential guide to squeezed Britain*, London: The Resolution Foundation.

[5] Oxley, M., Lishman, R., Brown, T., Haffner, M. and Hoekstra, J. (2010) *Promoting investment in private rented housing supply: international policy comparisons*, November, Department for Communities and Local Government. Available at: http://www.communities.gov.uk/publications/housing/investprivaterentedhousing

[6] McClure, K. (2011) *Reduction of worst case housing needs by assisted housing*, February, Washington, DC: US Department of Housing and Urban Development, Office of Policy Development and Research. This figure includes households with housing choice vouchers and those living in public housing and other federal project-based assistance programmes, as well as units built under the Low-Income Housing Tax Credit programme. See: http://www.huduser.org/portal/publications/ReductionofWCHNAssistedHousing.pdf

[7] Center for Housing Policy tabulations of the 2009 American Community Survey Public-Use Microdata Sample housing file.

[8] Marcus & Millichap Real Estate Investment Services (2011) 'Real estate investment research: national apartment report'. Available at: http://www.tcg-mm.com/marketresearch/MM2011NationalAptReport.pdf

[9] Joint Center for Housing Studies of Harvard University (2011) 'America's rental housing: meeting challenges, building on opportunities'. Available at: http://www.jchs.harvard.edu/sites/jchs.harvard.edu/files/americasrentalhousing-2011.pdf

[10] Marcus & Millichap Real Estate Investment Services (2011), op cit.

[11] Unless otherwise stated, information on affordable housing programmes was gathered from www.housingpolicy.org, a housing resource for practitioners developed and maintained by the Center for Housing Policy.

[12] States must give priority to projects with certain characteristics (eg projects affordable to tenants with the lowest incomes, projects with longer affordability periods, etc), but the QAP also allows states to specify additional selection criteria based on the location of the project, the population that it will serve and so on. See National Low Income Housing Coalition (2007) *The Qualified Allocation Plan: a potential tool in the affordable housing preservation toolbox*, February, Washington, DC: NLIHC.

[13] Novogradac & Company (2012) 'Resources: about the LIHTC'. Available at: http://www.novoco.com/low_income_housing/resources/program_summary.php (accessed 26 May 2011).

[14] Lawrence, P. (2011) 'Low Income Housing Tax Credit', in Clark, A. (ed) *2011 advocates' guide to housing & community development policy*, Washington, DC: National Low Income Housing Coalition, pp 133–6.

[15] Enterprise Community Investment, Inc. (2010) *Low-Income Housing Tax Credits: an investment that delivers more. To everyone*, Columbia, MD: Author.

[16] Ernst & Young LLP (2009) *Low-Income Housing Tax Credit investment survey*, October, Columbia, MD and New York, NY: Enterprise Community Partners, Inc. and Local Initiatives Support Corporation. Available at: http://www.ncsha.org/resource/ernst-young-low-income-housing-tax-credit-investment-survey

[17] Alakeson, V. (2011) *Making a rented house a home: housing solutions for generation rent*, London: The Resolution Foundation.

[18] Joint Center for Housing Studies of Harvard University (2011), op cit.

[19] Kimura, D. (2011) 'Looking for Balance', *Affordable Housing Finance*, September. Available at: http://www.housingfinance.com/ahf/articles/2011/september/0911-finance-Looking-for-Balance.htm (accessed 20 September 2011).

[20] Harper, D. (2011) 'How to analyze Real Estate Investment Trusts', Investopedia.com. Available at: http://www.investopedia.com/articles/04/030304.asp (accessed 27 May 2011).

[21] National Multihousing Council (2011) 'NMHC 50: a special supplement to national real estate investor', April. Available at: http://www.nmhc.org/Content/ServeFile.cfm?FileID=3523

[22] On its website, the Community Development Trust notes that it is 'the country's only private real estate investment trust with a public purpose', although this could not be independently verified. See: http://www.cdt.biz/whatwedo.htm (accessed 20 September 2011).

[23] Jones, C. (2007) 'Private investments in rented housing and the role of REITs', *European Journal of Housing Policy*, vol 7, no 4, pp 383-400.

[24] Center for Housing Policy (2011) 'Funding affordable homes through California's redevelopment process – an innovative and successful funding model', March. Available at: http://www.thecorecompanies.com/uploads/Redevelopment_brief_FINAL.pdf. Legislation passed in California in mid-2011 to address the state's significant budget deficit would, at a minimum, decrease the level of funding available to redevelopment agencies but could also dissolve the agencies entirely. The contested legislation, which is currently pending before the California Supreme Court, does not change the requirement that 20% of any TIF funds be used for affordable housing in the state.

[25] Information was gathered from conversations with Maine State Housing Authority staff and from the programme description, available at: http://www.mainehousing.org/TaxIncrement

[26] A summary of several studies suggests that growth within the TIF district does not lead to municipal-wide property value growth, and any localised increases may come at the expense of areas outside the district, particularly for commercial properties. See Dye, R.F. and Merriman, D.F. (2006) 'Tax increment financing: a tool for local economic development', *Land Lines*, vol 18, no 1, pp 2–8.

Insulating middle-income households from economic insecurity: why savings matter, and how we can increase them

Joanna Smith-Ramani and Preeti Mehta

There is a great deal of debate among economists about what impact the recession might have on household behaviour when it comes to saving, debts and spending. The optimists believe that households will continue to borrow to maintain their living standards in the face of rising prices and stagnant wages, fuelling a return to growth. Others are not so sure: they believe that households may start to rein in spending, reduce debt and begin to save more in the face of an uncertain economic future. Certainly, savings rates have increased since the downturn on both sides of the Atlantic. There is some evidence of households 'de-leveraging' – although some of this has been shown in the US to be the result of repossessions and defaults on loans – hardly signs of healthy household finances.

So, governments face a paradox: on the one hand, given that consumer spending accounts for approximately 70% of the economy, they need households to keep on spending to fuel the recovery – indeed, projections by the UK Office of Budgetary Responsibility build high levels of consumer borrowing into their forecasts. On the other hand, in an era of constrained public spending, both the US and UK governments are exhorting households to build up their own financial security so that they can weather economic shocks without resorting to relying on state support.

Taking a longer-term perspective, it is clear that since the 1970s, the US and the UK have become nations of spenders rather than savers. The UK household saving ratio plummeted from its peak of 12.3% in 1980 to just 1.7% in 2010, the lowest recorded figure since 1970, and substantially lower than the average of 7.6% recorded between 1970 and 2008. The US has exhibited similar patterns, with its saving ratio hitting an all-time low of 0.1% in 2008. Although it recovered somewhat from that nadir, reaching 5.3% by the end of 2010, this figure is still well below the normal levels for the 30 years before that.

At the same time as this long-term decline in household savings, debt as a proportion of household income has risen sharply when compared to 40-year patterns. Between 1994 and 2008, average family credit card debt in America doubled from US$4,300 to US$9,600.[1] US household debt hovered around 50% to 60% of total household income in the early 1970s; by 2007, it peaked at 135% of household income. The UK's borrowing habits are even more pronounced, with debt currently averaging 160% of household income.

This chapter argues that there is a strong case for supporting households to save more given the historically low levels of savings and the anticipated cuts in public supports in coming years. While the UK has extensive social safety nets that do not rely on individual savings, for example, free health care through the National Heath Service, it is clear that saving is both historically low in both countries and low by international standards. The chapter focuses specifically on short- and medium-term savings, rather than pensions and other forms of longer-term savings. This is not to dismiss the significance of longer-term savings for living standards, particularly in older age, but to recognise that different incentives and policy responses apply to pensions provision than to short- and medium-term savings. Drawing on our pioneering work at the Doorway to Dreams Fund (D2D) about what works, this chapter explores how low- and modest-income households can be better supported to save more.

We write at a time when the US policy world is littered with the debris of failed attempts to help low and modest earners build up assets. Historically, proposals designed to help lower-income families save have received less support than those that benefit middle- and higher-income households, such as Individual Retirement Accounts and 401(k)s.

Account-based proposals such as Clinton's Universal Savings Accounts (USAs) never received the backing they needed to become reality. Proposals designed to help lower-income families at the state level have largely been anti-poverty programmes such as Temporary Assistance for Needy Families (TANF). Individual Development Accounts (IDAs) have been the only account-based systems implemented at the state level. As we explore later on, these programmes have had difficulty reaching scale. And now, it looks like history will repeat itself: the Obama administration introduced the Americans Savings for Personal Investment, Retirement, and Education Act (the ASPIRE Act) to both the House and the Senate in 2010. This Bill would provide an account for every child born in America. But it has not been acted upon.

In all these cases, the main barriers have not been policy-driven. Both the USA account proposal and the ASPIRE Act were expensive proposals. Rather, in a climate that favours small government, there has been little or no political appetite to stomach large budget programmes such as these.

Assets have long been underplayed by those campaigning for improving the economic opportunities available to low- and modest-income households. This chapter highlights some of the most exciting innovations that have been successfully trialled in the US in recent years. The task now is to find ways of taking these innovations to scale, via government and the private sector.

The difference that savings can make

Savings offer vital insulation against shocks. A Consumer Federation of America survey found that families with just US$500 in emergency savings had better financial outcomes than moderate-income households with lower savings. This finding is significant at a time when economic circumstances are leaving many households highly exposed: 16% of Americans are working fewer hours than they would like and the unemployment rate is still hovering at 9%. Unemployment and underemployment are also major challenges for families in the UK. Job insecurity on both sides of the Atlantic is compounded by rising living costs, and in the UK specifically, cuts to the tax credits and benefits that have made up an increasingly significant part of family budgets over the last decade. So, more than ever before, savings are key to the economic security of low- and modest-income households.

But savings are not simply an immediate stop-gap for families, important though that is. Research has shown that they have a longer-term impact on the life chances of children too. More than 50% of Americans who start out in the lowest income bracket remain there if their parents have low savings – but only 29% remain there if their parents have high savings.[2] Financial capital, along with family structure and educational attainment, are the three strongest predictors of economic mobility in the US.

In other words, savings not only help to lower the chances of a family moving downwards, but they can also increase social and economic mobility. Savings enable people to seize opportunities, such as relocating for a job, retraining or starting up a new business. This evidence underpinned the Labour government's asset-based welfare policies in the UK, notably, the creation the Child Trust Fund that has since been scrapped by the Coalition government.

Given the significance of savings to family well-being, it is concerning that savings activity is even more unevenly distributed in the UK than is income. The gini co-efficient for 'financial wealth' (which includes non-pension savings) is 0.81, higher than it is even for property wealth and pensions wealth. The bottom 50% of the population owns just 1% of total net financial wealth, while the top 20% owns 84%. A quarter of households have net financial wealth that is negligible.[3]

The general consensus among financial advisers is that 'adequate' savings should equate to being able to survive for three months without income. And yet Resolution Foundation analysis shows that two thirds of low- to middle-income households in the UK have less than £1,500 saved up. Over half of this group do not have enough savings to cover a month's gross income, and nearly three quarters have less than two months' earnings in the bank.[4] This is evidence that those households most at risk of unemployment, underemployment and other income shocks are also the households least able to accumulate savings.

Three innovations that support saving activity

The UK Financial Services Authority baseline survey of financial capability underlined an important point: that whatever their household circumstances or income level, humans are universally poor at 'planning ahead'. Too few people are saving, either for a rainy day or for later life.

Less well-off households are no different than other households in this weakness at planning ahead. However, they have more pronounced challenges when it comes to saving. Many low earners are living on the edge, just about balancing income and outgoings each month but with very little money left over to set aside – the reason given by the majority of this group for not saving, or not saving more. Furthermore, the market for financial products and services that suit their needs remains underdeveloped and heavily dependent on government subsidy. Market failures are compounded by insufficient or poorly targeted public policies and patchy financial education.

Despite these challenges, our work at D2D shows that low- and modest-income households can and do save when given the right opportunities. Financial innovations can be tailored to the specific needs of these households and designed to address these challenges. As this typology shows,[5] these innovations span a spectrum from requiring people to save, to making saving fun:

1. Coercing Saving.
2. Making it Hard *Not* to Save.
3. Making it Easier to Save.
4. Providing Incentives, or Bribing People to Save.
5. Making Saving a Group Activity (Social Support Networks).
6. Making Saving Fun and Exciting.

There are examples of financial innovations in each of these categories that are making a positive difference across the US. Here, we draw out a handful of the most impactful and promising innovations of recent years, which will be of interest to British policymakers.

Making it easier to save: using the tax credit system

The interest in 'nudge'[6] and behavioural economics has spawned a range of financial innovations on both sides of the Atlantic. The big idea of nudge is to create defaults or systems that make it difficult to choose *not* to save. Good examples in the UK are the Save As You Earn scheme, whereby workers can elect to deduct money for savings directly from their salary, so that it never hits their current accounts; more recently, the 'opt-out' design of the National Employment Savings Trust (NEST) pension scheme should increase take-up and address the worryingly low levels of retirement savings.

One of the most exciting innovations of this field in recent years in the US is the Tax Time Savings Bond, announced by President Obama at the end of 2009, and coordinated by D2D and the Savings Bond Working Group. This policy has a simple ambition: to encourage 1 million Americans to invest a part of their tax credit into a Savings Bond each year. Already, 45,000 people have generated US$11 million of savings through this initiative.

The design of the scheme is simple. Each year, Americans file a tax return. Tax credits are paid as a lump sum, based on the previous year's income and household composition. Since 2010, there has been an option on the tax form for filers to check if they wish to invest some of their tax credit payment into a Savings Bond. They can also opt to 'gift' the Savings Bond to others, such as children or grandchildren.

The number of Tax Time Bond buyers has risen dramatically, from 1,708 in 2009 (the last year of the D2D pilot) to 45,000 in 2011, and we have already learnt a great deal from the scheme that is significant for future innovations:

- Tax Time Saving appears to be habit-forming, with early data showing that more than a quarter who chose to save in 2010 did so again in 2011 – despite the challenges of the recession.
- Nearly half of all tax time savers in 2011 chose to save on behalf of others, a finding corroborated by Tax Time Savings pilots that D2D and others conducted between 2007 and 2009.
- Poorer households benefit the most from this policy, with early 2011 data showing that more than 80% of the savers had below median household incomes. Given the difficulties these households have in finding money for savings from daily and weekly budgets, this suggests that Tax Time Saving is highly effective relative to other innovations.

The major difference between tax credits in the US and the UK is that in the US they are paid as a lump sum annually, rather than on a monthly basis. However, as the UK government redesigns the tax credit and benefit system, there is an opportunity to consider whether or how any payments might be made as a lump sum, with savings opportunities attached. Equally, there is an opportunity to consider whether the same principle behind the Savings Bond scheme could be applied to monthly tax credit payments. Already, some UK credit unions work with customers to deduct debt repayments from their tax credits or welfare benefits. This model could be developed further to focus on savings too.

Providing incentives: Individual Development Accounts

The principle underpinning IDAs – that matched contributions would help low- and modest-income households to save – was first proposed in Michael Sherraden's landmark work *Assets and the poor* in 1991.[7] Since then, there has been considerable interest in the concept globally. In the US, Sherraden's work inspired a handful of non-governmental organisations (NGOs) to organise some small pilots of match-funded schemes during the 1990s.

From these humble beginnings, IDAs have expanded rapidly, receiving their first dedicated federal funding in 1998. By 2009, there were just over 60,000 accounts held nationally. Account-holders had deposited US$56.5 million in earned income – an average of US$943 per account-holder.[8] There are two distinctive features shared by all IDA products: first, the match is contingent upon savings being used for a significant asset, such as buying a home, entering higher education or starting a business; and, second, participants are all required to go through financial education programmes.

IDAs have certainly proved effective in helping to meet some of the saving needs of low- and modest-earning Americans. However, the strict limits on what the funds can be used for put some people off, and meant that IDAs cannot help low earners weather unexpected costs. Additionally, the model built in the US is challenging to scale across the country. For that reason, we looked on with envy at the UK's Child Trust Fund and Savings Gateway – two matched funding schemes introduced under the last government with no restrictions on how the money was spent.

Our experience at D2D suggests that the abolition of scaled-up match-funded offerings such as the Child Trust Fund – replaced now with a Junior Individual Saving Account (ISA) product – will be a step backwards when it comes to supporting low-earning households to save. While the IDA scheme is far from perfect, its underlying principle of match-funding makes a much bigger difference to poorer households than incentives offered through the tax system, as is the case with ISAs. The US picture offers a particularly pronounced illustration of this: US$340 billion was allocated through the federal tax code to support saving in the financial year of 2011, and half of this expenditure goes into the pockets of the richest 5% of US taxpayers.[9]

The UK is not immune from the unfair effects of tax incentives to save. Tax relief on ISAs – owned by just 29% of British people – cost £1.6 billion in 2009/10, three times as much as the £520 million cost of the Child Trust Fund that year. In 2005, it was estimated that 60% of all tax relief on savings went to higher-rate taxpayers.[10] While this figure is likely to have fallen recently, thanks to changes to pension tax relief, it remains the case that lower-income households will gain much less from such tax-based strategies. In progressive tax systems, tax-based incentives will always disproportionately benefit higher earners.

Even if these concerns about unfairness are set aside, there are still strong arguments to favour match-funding schemes over tax incentives to support low-earner households to save. In a UK study that corroborates our own US-based research, Kempson and Finney found that of all financial incentives to save, tax relief was the least appealing to low earners.[11]

Making saving fun and exciting: prize-linked savings

The UK Premium Bonds scheme has over 20 million participants who collectively hold over £25 billion of savings. Our recent work at D2D underlines the huge potential of such 'prize-linked savings' schemes as part of a wider strategy to support greater saving activity among low- and modest-income households. Prize-linked savings offer a return to participants in the form of a chance to win large prizes, rather than in more traditional forms of interest or capital accumulation.

Prize-linked savings schemes face varying regulatory and legal challenges in the US, depending on the structure and sponsor of the product. However, a recent D2D pilot with eight Michigan credit unions shows just what an impact such schemes can have. Within the first year of the programme, 11,600 residents opened a 'Save to Win' account for the chance of winning a monthly prize, or an annual prize of US$100,000. Between them, they saved US$8.6 million. Of the participating savers, 44% earned less than US$40,000 a year, and 45% of them were non-regular savers. Data for 2010 continue to demonstrate use of this product by low- and moderate-income consumers as well as non-savers.[12]

The findings of this pilot underline earlier research conducted in Indiana, which indicated that prize-linked savings schemes appeal much more to lower than higher earners, with people with assets of below US$2000 2.5 times more interested than people with more than US$50,000 in assets. Non-savers were also more predisposed to the scheme, as were regular lottery players. With Americans spending US$80 billion on legalised forms of gambling (including the lottery) in 2003, even a small substitution effect between lottery spending and a prize-linked savings scheme would significantly increase aggregate savings.[13]

As Peter Tufano, Dean of the Said Business School, has argued, prize-linked savings are 'a textbook application of certain behavioural economics principles'.[14] Such products blend the guarantee of no loss with a large, albeit low-probability, gain. Furthermore, they have a strong appeal for low-earning households. One recent survey showed that a fifth of all Americans, and nearly two in five people with incomes below US$25,000, believe that 'winning the lottery' is the most realistic chance they have of building substantial assets.[15]

Aside from their popularity with the target group, there are other good reasons to make more of prize-linked saving schemes as a route to increasing the savings of low-earning households. First, in an era of fiscal austerity and public sector cuts, they do not require public subsidies or taxpayer expenses. Second, they have many potential applications. For example, Washington Mutual and JP Chase Bank offered savers a chance to double their deposits, creating three winners each month, up to the value of US$10,000, and UK banks have created similar opportunities for savers. Employers offering pension or health schemes could incorporate a similar principle to attract low-earning employees, who typically are less likely to join such schemes. State-sponsored lotteries could link the promise of winning to savings behaviour.

In the US, we have an uphill struggle to remove the legal barriers to enabling more prize-linked saving activity. Other than the legal barriers faced in the US, perhaps the biggest roadblock facing prize-linked programmes is the challenge of getting to scale. In contrast, the UK already has an infrastructure in place in the form of the Premium Bonds scheme. Our work in the US suggests that there remains huge untapped potential in this model, and that the UK could do much more to integrate prize-linked savings into a wider strategy for supporting saving among low- and modest-income households.

Conclusion

Saving is a challenge for everyone. It requires discipline, planning, optimism about the future and access to a good product at the right time. Saving implies one has money left over to save after expenses and other obligations. In other words, the barriers to saving involve a range of factors, from personal outlooks to market failures. In this complex picture, government is one player among many. Financial services, non-profits and supermarkets are just a few of the other actors who play a potential role in encouraging greater savings among poorer households.

That said, the government's role as a market-shaper is critical. It is in a unique position to develop supportive policies and regulation and to convene the key players. Therefore, it is vital that the government fully comprehends the potential impact of different interventions designed to support more saving activity among low earners. As this chapter has shown, there are some programmes that are likely to be more successful than others, but what we also know is that there is not a single initiative that will meet the saving needs of low-earning households.

A 'dream' recovery from the recession would involve an increase in consumer spending at the same time as a reduction in household debt. While there is some evidence that households are beginning to save more, it remains the case that the majority of low- to modest-income households on both sides of the Atlantic have inadequate savings, and that they are more exposed now than ever before, thanks to rising job insecurity, increases in the costs of living and cuts in public expenditure. Finding ways of increasing the savings of these families would be great news for a balanced recovery. And given the evidence that assets breed social mobility, it would be even better news for low- and modest-income households.

Notes

[1] Doorways to Dreams (D2D) Fund (2011) 'Policy update'. Available at: http://www.d2dfund.org/files/publications/D2Dbrief.pdf

[2] Isaacs, J. (2007) 'Economic mobility of families across generations', The Economic Mobility Project. Available at: http://www.economicmobility.org/assets/pdfs/EMP_FamiliesAcrossGenerations_ChapterI.pdf

[3] Daffin, G. (2009) 'Wealth in Britain. Main Results from the Wealth and Assets Survey 2006/08', Office for National Statistics. Available at: http://www.google.co.uk/url?sa=t&rct=j&q=&esrc=s&source=web&cd=2&ved=0CEYQFjAB&url=http%3A%2F%2Fwww.ons.gov.uk%2Fons%2Frel%2Fwas%2Fwealth-in-great-britain%2Fmain-results-from-the-wealth-and-assets-survey-2006-2008%2Freport--wealth-in-great-britain-.pdf&ei=UGcuUJrkAciZhQeAoYFo&usg=AFQjCNHl5z1nJGJyht1GJRxMahjJMLeZ-A&cad=rja

[4] Parker, S. (2010) 'Behind the balance sheet: the financial health of low income households', Resolution Foundation. Available at: http://www.resolutionfoundation.org/publications/behind-balance-sheet-financial-health-low-income-h/

[5] Adapted from Tufano, P. and Schneider, D. (2008) 'Using financial innovation to support savers: from coercion to excitement', National Poverty Center policy brief no. 14. Available at: http://www.npc.umich.edu/publications/policy_briefs/brief14/index.php

[6] Thaler, R. and Sunstein, C. (2008) *Nudge: improving decisions about health, wealth and happiness*, New Haven, CT: Yale University Press.

[7] Sherraden, M. (1992) *Assets and the poor: the new American welfare policy.* Armont, NY: M.E. Sharpe.

[8] From US Department of Health and Human Services (2009) 'Assets for Independence Program: status at the conclusion of the tenth year'. Available at: http://www.acf.hhs.gov/programs/ocs/afi/AFITenthReporttoCongress.pdf

[9] Woo, B., Rademacher, I. and Meier, J. (2010) 'Upside down: the $400 billion federal asset-building budget', CFED/Annie E. Casey Foundation. Available at: http://www.aecf.org/KnowledgeCenter/Publications.aspx?pubguid={6D62ACDE-6BAC-4000-A356-5185344AFC46}

[10] Dolphin, T. (2011) 'Designing a life-course savings account', Institute for Public Policy Research. Available at: http://www.ippr.org/research-projects/44/7128/designing-a-life-course-savings-account

[11] Kempson, E. and Finney, A. (2009) *Saving in lower-income households: an evidence review for the Financial Inclusion Taskforce,* quoted in Dolphin (2011), ibid.

[12] See D2D Fund (2011) 'A win-win for all: the growth of Save to Win in Michigan'. Available at: http://www.d2dfund.org/files/publications/11_STW2011_Report_lo-res_single.pdf

[13] Tufano, P., Maynard, N. and De Neve, J. (2008) 'Consumer demand for prize-linked savings: a preliminary analysis', HBS Working Paper. Available at: http://www.hbs.edu/research/pdf/08-061.pdf

[14] Tufano, P. (2008) 'Saving whilst gambling: an empirical analysis of UK Premium Bonds', *American Economic Review,* May (Papers and Proceedings).

[15] Quoted in Tufano et al (2008), op cit. Available at: http://www.people.hbs.edu/ptufano/Whilst.pdf

Section 3

Looking ahead: a cautionary tale

The path to post-recession prosperity

Tamara Draut

Austerity or prosperity?

With the UK economy experiencing a double-dip recession, more questions are now being asked about the merits of the Chancellor's view that there is no alternative to the current austerity plan. The package of spending cuts and tax rises introduced to tackle the deficit over the last two years represent the tightest five-year squeeze on public service spending since the Second World War.[1] UK public spending is projected to be lower than the US's as a percentage of gross domestic product (GDP) by 2015.[2] The UK government's austerity measures aim, by 2015/16, to eliminate the deficit altogether, and to ensure that public sector debt has started to fall from its projected peak of 70.9% of GDP in 2013/14.[3]

And yet what the UK and the US face today more closely resembles a 'lost decade' than a 'burst bubble'. The proposed austerity measures fail to capture this truth. Even if cuts did return our economies to growth – and there is little sign of a private sector-led recovery at present – there is scant evidence that recovery alone will address the long-term squeeze in living standards being felt by low-earning households on both sides of the Atlantic.

While newly elected leaders in France and Greece are setting out alternative economic plans for the eurozone countries, turning away from strict adherence to deficit reduction, the UK is not alone in its focus on austerity. Indeed, it has become the primary framework by which congressional leaders are considering both short-term and long-term plans for the US's economic future. Despite the failure of the bipartisan Joint Select Committee to reach agreement at the end of 2011 on a final package of austerity measures, Democrats and Republicans alike have accepted the need to take US$4 trillion out of the deficit over the next decade. The issue is how to do this fairly and sustainably, and who should shoulder the burden of the pain from such draconian cuts.

Much of the debate in the US to date has focused on non-military discretionary spending – the money we spend on education, green energy, national parks, transport and so on. These are vital services but together represent just 12% of total government spending. Republicans have proposed swingeing cuts to these budgets while maintaining the Bush tax cuts at a cost of over US$1 trillion. The Democrats have a battle on their hands to widen the debate about austerity measures to consider *all* discretionary government expenditure – including spending in the form of tax breaks – if they are to ensure that vital services are not cut at the same time that the tax code continues to disproportionately benefit the wealthy.

Last year, Demos, the Economic Policy Institute and The Century Foundation developed a blueprint for a fiscal future for the US that would meet the crucial goals of greater investment, deficit reduction and putting the nation's debt on a sustainable path. This blueprint – which has been scored by an independent organisation – starts with a deeper truth that we believe has been lost in the febrile debates about austerity measures.[4]

That truth is that the living standards crisis for low-earning households began several decades ago. As Heidi Sheirholz and Larry Mishel highlight in Chapter 1.1 of this volume, it is no longer the case in the US that each generation is better off than the last. The UK has also witnessed the stagnation of median wages and the failure of pay to keep up with productivity since 2003.

This means that instead of their narrow goal of delivering austerity measures, leaders in the UK and the US must focus urgently on rebuilding the middle class, and the pathways into the middle class. At this time of prolonged and sustained joblessness, stagnating earnings and growing economic insecurity, what is needed is a commitment to the type of public investments that fuelled the broad economic expansion in the post-war years.

This is not to say that today's strategies should mimic those of the 1950s and 1960s – it is a decidedly different context in which our economy operates. Yet, the basic strategy of robust public investment and a progressive and fair revenue system are relevant, and in some ways more critical, today. In order to compete globally and sustain a broad middle class, we need again to embark on a set of strategies to fuel growth, reduce debt and create widely shared prosperity.

As we argue in our blueprint, to build that platform for sustained growth requires a full recovery from the recession, which means getting people back to work. Beyond this, there are two priorities, as this chapter describes: first, a more sustainable balance between spending cuts and tax rises; and, second, a plan for longer-term investments that will lay the foundation for broad-based prosperity by successfully creating jobs for middle-class workers. These priorities should apply to the UK as much as they do to the US – and represent an alternative path to recovery from the austerity measures that are currently driving the administrations on either side of the Atlantic.

The revenue path to prosperity

As the furious debates in Congress in 2011 suggest, tax is a contentious issue in the US, even more so than in the UK. To make the investments required to rebuild the middle class, the US will need to find a way to replenish its revenue base, which has fallen as a result of changes in tax policy over the last decade, and has been exacerbated by the recession. We are unique among developed nations in terms of how much we spend through the tax code: tax breaks make up 2% of GDP, and disproportionately benefit the rich. Reducing this expenditure, as well as making strategic cuts to defence spending, would be a much fairer way of making savings than cutting and compromising vital public services.

Federal tax revenue is lower than it has been in half a century. The federal government's revenues from income taxes on households make up 6.4% of GDP – 3.8 percentage points lower than the peak in the boom year of 2000.[5] Corporate income taxes, at 1% of GDP, are 6.2 percentage points lower than their apex in 1945. Our current tax revenues are not only low relative to historical levels, but they rank low internationally as well. Our total tax revenues, including federal, state and local taxes, comprise 27% of GDP, a level far lower than the UK and, indeed, most of our peers in the developed world.[6] Among the 33 nations of the Organisation for Economic Co-operation and Development (OECD), only three (Korea, Turkey and Mexico) take in proportionately less tax revenue than the US does.

So, the US is in many ways unique when it comes to its tax system. Over the years, differences have become even more pronounced, as tax rates for the rich have been cut. The current marginal tax rate for the highest income bracket of 35% is among the lowest since the Second World War,[7] and the effective tax rate – the actual percentage of a household's entire income paid in taxes – for the rich has also fallen precipitously, dropping from 31.3% for millionaires in 1993 to 22% today.[8] The tax rate on profits earned from the sale of investments in capital, such as stocks, bonds or real estate, has fallen even faster than the tax rate on wage income. From a post-war high of nearly 40% in 1978, the tax rate for capital gains now stands at an all-time low of 15%.[9]

Falling tax rates are not the only causes of the decline in effective tax rates. The federal government lost US$878 billion in revenue in 2008[10] from individual income tax deductions and credits given out for a variety of incentives including mortgage interest deductions for owner-occupied homes and tax-free employer contributions for health insurance.[11] The benefits from these tax breaks, collectively referred to as tax expenditures, disproportionately flow to upper-income households. Tax deductions for mortgage interest and retirement plan contributions are two of the most unequal, with roughly two thirds of the tax savings from these benefits accruing to the highest-earning 20% of households.

The gross unfairness designed into the US tax system is not reflected to anywhere near the same extent in the UK system. In fact, reforms since 1997 have been broadly progressive, with the poorest 10% of households gaining, on average, an amount equal to 12.8% of their income and the richest 10% of households losing an amount equal to about 8.7% of their net incomes.[12] When it comes to tax expenditures, mortgage interest relief has been eliminated. There have been attempts to make tax relief on pensions more progressive in recent years – although the fact is that it remains deeply regressive.

Despite this more progressive backdrop, the austerity measures set out in the UK's 2011 Budget are cause for concern. The Institute for Fiscal Studies has shown that, collectively, these measures will hit lower-earning households harder than their better-off counterparts. Our blueprint argues that there are no pain-free solutions for making the necessary savings, but the least-damaging options from the perspective of low and modest earners are progressive taxes on income and wealth, rather than indirect taxes, sharpening of tapers or cuts to services. There remains a much better balance to be struck in the UK's plans between cutting spending and raising tax revenue. These options must be part of the public debate about deficit reduction if we are to return to 'good growth' and broad-based prosperity.

The spending path to prosperity

In the last 30 years, the US has experienced a paradox of productivity and progress. Productivity, driven by extraordinary growth in technology and an increased push towards consumption, has nearly tripled. Meanwhile social, environmental and educational progress has stalled. We are not only experiencing a crisis in jobs, but also in investment – in both physical and human capital – which, in turn, is dragging down our economic growth. Indeed, economist David Aschauer has shown that more than half of the decline in productivity growth that began in the early 1970s could be attributed to reduced public investment.[13]

Investment in social and human capital provides major returns in terms of economic growth. For example, one study found that providing universal early years services, at a cost of roughly US$40 billion annually, could provide net benefits leading to GDP being roughly 2% higher in 2045 than it would be without this investment – a pay-off of nearly eight to one.[14] Similarly, spending on public infrastructure – transportation, energy, water systems and public buildings, for example – has historically been a driver of economic growth.[15] Such investments in infrastructure are an extremely efficient way of creating jobs, which, in turn, generate economic growth nationally while providing employment and stability to thousands of middle-class households.

Our blueprint explores various costed options for investment to generate fair growth. In this chapter, we consider two issues specifically, as illustrations of this broader point: investing in childcare as a form of human and social capital; and investing in physical infrastructure as a stimulus to jobs and, ultimately, growth.

Investing in childcare

Most developed nations have recognised that affordable childcare is both a necessity for working parents and a key investment in the cognitive and social development of children. Childcare matters especially for middle-class households, where women's entry into the labour market since the middle of the 20th century has been key to sustaining household incomes in an era of male wage stagnation. Failure to provide affordable childcare that fits with modern working patterns leaves middle-class living standards at risk: if care is too expensive, work no longer pays. Too many middle-class families today are in a catch-22 situation: forced to choose between spending significant proportions of their wages on childcare costs, or forgoing one person's salary in order that they can stay at home to look after the children.

On the face of it, the US and the UK are alike in spending more on child welfare and education as a proportion of GDP than other OECD countries. However, taking a more in-depth look shows that much of this spending in the US goes to public compulsory education rather than early years support and childcare. This flies in the face of evidence that the effectiveness of public investment in human capital is higher when it takes place in the pre-school years.[16]

For example, in 2005, total public spending in the US on child care and pre-school was 0.4% of GDP, ranking 28th out of 37 countries.[17] Childcare assistance is provided to only about one in seven children who are eligible to receive federal assistance.[18] A significant proportion of family support is strongly linked to employment, with 45% of total support in the US being delivered through tax breaks and credits (compared to just 10% on average across OECD countries) – meaning that richer families benefit disproportionately more from spending. Childcare coverage is patchy and of mixed quality[19] and there is no national paid parental leave policy. Investing properly in a high-quality early care system to serve the 25 million American children aged five and under would average US$88 billion a year – a significant sum, but in this context, it is one that would yield even more significant returns, as Lane Kenworthy shows in Chapter 1.2 of this volume.

In contrast, the UK has seen a decade of investment in early years and family support, heavily targeted towards poorer families. As a result, the UK is now one of the biggest investors in families across the OECD. Public spending on family benefits stood at 3.6% of GDP in 2007, compared to an OECD average of 2.2%, and an American investment of just 1.2% of GDP.

Despite the UK's impressive track record in this area, there is little room for complacency. Childcare in the UK remains among the most expensive in the OECD, accounting for a quarter of average family household income in 2004, compared to just 16% across the OECD. This has a negative impact on work incentives for second earners: over two thirds of their income is taxed away upon entering work, once childcare costs are taken into account.[20] It is perhaps not surprising that full-time work among mothers is lower in the UK than the OECD average.

This presents a challenge to the UK government as it develops its policies for childcare as part of the move towards the Universal Credit from 2013. Childcare support has already been cut as part of the austerity measures, costing families an estimated average of £436 each year.[21] While the government is committed to maintaining childcare spending at £2 billion a year under the Universal Credit scheme, it is also committed to widening eligibility. The risk is that these two commitments combine to leave individual families worse off than before – at a time when household budgets are already being squeezed by stagnant wages and rising costs.

Investing in physical infrastructure

Maintaining a physical infrastructure as large as that in the US is a formidable challenge, and one that we have not met. Even when combining federal, state, local and private sector expenditures, the US currently spends about 2% of GDP per year on infrastructure investment. This is well below the average of what other developed nations spend (3%) and significantly less than the estimated nine-plus percent spent by China.[22]

Our level of investment is inadequate to keep much of our current infrastructure functioning, let alone to improve it.[23] Beyond these concerns, there is a strong case for public investment in infrastructure as a mechanism for job creation. Never has the need for effective job creation policies been more pressing: the US unemployment rate has doubled from 2007 figures, and since 2009, it has hovered at 9%. Without such policies, it seems unlikely that the recovery will yield the kind of growth that will stabilise the middle class and secure their living standards.

There has been much research and academic debate about the relative effectiveness of different forms of public expenditure, as measured by the number of jobs created per US$1 billion of spending. For example, cash benefits are perceived to offer a good 'bang-per-buck', as their recipients are likely to spend the money they receive. In contrast, tax cuts appear to be a less effective mechanism, as recipients are more likely to save some or all of the cut.

Spending on public infrastructure has been shown to have a multiplier effect of 1.44, making it a highly effective engine of job creation. Heintz et al estimate that every US$1 billion of new investment spending creates 18,000 jobs – 22% more jobs than if that US$1 billion had been spent on a tax cut. These jobs are created in three key ways:[24]

- Direct jobs: in manufacturing, construction and so on.
- Indirect jobs: in sectors and industries that produce the supplies purchased by infrastructure projects.
- Induced jobs: these are the jobs created as a result of an overall rise in spending as more people enter employment – for example, in the retail and food industries.

As well as having a high 'bang-per-buck', economists suggest that such stimulus spending is partially self-financing, with each dollar of infrastructure spending raising $0.53 of revenue.[25] In this context, the Obama Administration's 'Jobs Plan', launched in 2011, is good news, not only for middle-class families in need of employment, but also for the economy as a whole. It must draw on the evidence about which interventions work, and which of them will make an immediate difference in order to avoid the risk of a double-dip recession.

There are many different proposals already on the table for job creation programmes that also revitalise the crumbling infrastructure of the US. Of these, perhaps the most important are projects that invest in clean energy sources. Our current approach to power generation and usage is not sustainable, in every sense of the word. In 2009, China invested nearly US$35 billion in clean energy, close to double the US$19 billion invested by the US. The Recovery Act of 2009 did more than ever before in this sphere, but further work is needed. A US$200 billion investment would create 2.1 million jobs each year, as well as reducing energy costs and dependency on foreign oil.[26]

In the past, the UK has taken investment in public infrastructure much more seriously than the US. For over a decade, the Labour administrations increased capital expenditure, rolling out major infrastructure projects in transportation, energy, broadband and public buildings. And yet from 2009, with very little public debate, these investments were cut dramatically. Capital investment is projected to tumble from £70 billion in 2010 to £46 billion by the middle of the decade.

In other words, while the US needs to find new ways of investing in public infrastructure, it is equally pressing that UK policymakers find ways of restoring previous levels of expenditure on capital investment as one of the most effective mechanisms for job creation. There is no question that both countries face formidable infrastructure needs in the 21st century, from housing, to renewable energy, to transportation. As Gavin Kelly and Nick Pearce have argued, 'a pro-stability, growth and full employment agenda must put productive investment first'.[27]

Conclusion

There are of course some important differences in the context of austerity programmes in the UK and the US. Living standards have been in decline for longer in the US, and median wage stagnation is more pronounced. The social contract of the US is threadbare: when it comes to social spending, we rank 27th out of all 34 OECD countries. The US lacks a national health system, instead relying on a private health insurance system in which premiums and out-of-pocket expenses have outpaced inflation for some years now.

Notwithstanding these differences, both countries are in danger of putting austerity before prosperity. This may be ideologically appealing but the economics are less clear-cut, particularly given that private sector investment has been slow to restart given ongoing instability in the eurozone countries. There is no question that difficult decisions about spending cuts will need to be made to reduce the deficit. But such proposals must be put in the context not only of the recession, but also of the deeper and longer-term crisis in living standards for low- and middle-income households.

The task of fiscal balancing must put broad-based prosperity – not recovery and deficit reduction alone – at its heart. And that means rebuilding a strong middle class. To achieve this, as well as painful spending cuts, our leaders must consider how to usher in fair and progressive taxation systems, alongside renewed investment in the public services and infrastructure designed to provide economic security and opportunity to low-earning households.

Notes

[1] Institute for Fiscal Studies (2009) 'Loosening public service squeeze requires tax rises or welfare cuts'. Available at: http://www.ifs.org.uk/pr/fiscal_squeeze. pdf

[2] Taylor-Gooby, P. and Stoker, G. (2011) 'The Coalition programme: a new vision for Britain or politics as usual?', *The Political Quarterly*, vol 82, no 1, pp 4–15.

[3] Office of Budgetary Responsibility (2011) 'Economic and fiscal outlook March 2011'. Available at: http://budgetresponsibility.independent.gov.uk/ wordpress/docs/economic_and_fiscal_outlook_23032011.pdf

[4] To read more about this blueprint, see: http://www.ourfiscalsecurity.org/ storage/Blueprint_OFS.pdf

[5] Office of Management and Budget (2009) 'Historical tables, budget of the United States government', Table 2.3. Available at: http://www.whitehouse. gov/omb/budget/Historicals/

[6] Organisation for Economic Co-operation and Development (2010) 'Tax database Table O.1'. Available at: http://www.oecd.org/document/60/0,33 43,en_2649_34533_1942460_1_1_1_1,00.html#trs

[7] Tax Policy Center (2009) 'Tax facts: historical individual income tax parameters', 29 October. Available at: http://www.taxpolicycenter.org/ taxfacts/displayafact.cfm?Docid=543

[8] Internal Revenue Service (1993–2007) 'Individual income tax returns publication1304'. Available at: http://www.irs.gov/taxstats/indtaxstats/article/0,,id=134951,00.html

[9] Citizens for Tax Justice (2004) 'Top federal income tax rates on regular income and capital gains since 1916', May. Available at: http://www.ctj.org/pdf/regcg.pdf

[10] Burman, L., Toder, E. and Geissler, C. (2008) 'How big are total individual tax expenditures and who benefits from them?', Tax Policy Center, December. Available at: http://www.taxpolicycenter.org/UploadedPDF/1001234_tax_expenditures.pdf

[11] Office of Management and Budget (2009) 'Analytical perspectives: budget of the U.S. government 2010', US Government Printing Office. Available at: http://www.gpoaccess.gov/usbudget/fy10/pdf/spec.pdf

[12] Browne, J. and Phillips, D. (2010) *Tax and benefit reforms under Labour*, London: Institute for Fiscal Studies.

[13] Aschauer, D.A. (1989) 'Does public capital crowd out private capital?', *Journal of Monetary Economics*, vol 2, no 42, pp 171–88; Aschauer, D.A. (1989) 'Is public expenditure productive?', *Journal of Monetary Economics*, vol 2, no 32, pp 177–200; Aschauer, D.A. (1989) 'Public investment and productivity growth in the group of seven', *Economic Perspectives*, vol 1, no 35, pp 17–25; Aschauer, D.A. (1990) *Public investment and private sector growth*, Washington, DC: Economic Policy Institute.

[14] Lynch, R.G. (2007) *Enriching children, enriching the nation: public investment in high-quality prekindergarten*, Washington, DC: Economic Policy Institute.

[15] Heintz, J., Pollin, R. and Garrett-Peltier, R. (2009) *How infrastructure investments support the US economy: employment, productivity and growth*, Amherst, MA: Political Economy Research Institute, UMass.

[16] OECD (2011) 'Doing better for families'. Available at: http://www.oecd.org/document/49/0,3746,en_2649_34819_47654961_1_1_1_1,00.html#press

[17] OECD (2011) 'PF3.1: Public spending on childcare and early education', OECD Family Database. Available at: http://www.oecd.org/dataoecd/44/20/38954032.xls

[18] Mezey, J., Greenberg, M. and Schumacher, R. (2002) 'The vast majority of federally eligible children did not receive child care assistance in FY 2000', Center for Law and Social Policy. Available at: http://www.clasp.org/publications/1in7full.pdf

[19] The National Women's Law Center found that payment rates to providers serving children receiving childcare assistance are 'far too low to support good-quality care'. National Women's Law Center (2010) 'Letter to Joseph Biden', 25 February. Available at: www.whitehouse.gov/sites/default/files/microsites/100226-child-care.pdf

[20] OECD (2011), op cit, n 16.

[21] Alakeson, V. (2011) 'Childcare: failing to meet the needs of working parents', Resolution Foundation. Available at: http://www.resolutionfoundation.org/publications/childcare-failing-meet-needs-working-parents/

[22] Milano, J. (2009) 'Building America's 21st century infrastructure', Progressive Policy Institute. Available at: http://www.policyarchive.org/handle/10207/bitstreams/11834.pdf

[23] The American Society of Civil Engineers estimates that we will need to invest an additional US$1.1 billion over the next five years in order to adequately improve the condition of our infrastructure.

[24] Heintz et al (2009), op cit.

[25] Eisenbrey, R., Mishel, L., Bivens, J. and Fieldhouse, A. (2011) 'Policies for job creation and stronger economic growth', Economic Policy Institute. Available at: http://w3.epi-data.org/temp2011/BriefingPaper325.pdf

[26] Walsh, J., Bivens, J. and Pollock, E. (2011) 'Rebuilding green: the American Recovery and Reinvestment Act and the green economy', BlueGreen Alliance. Available at: http://www.bluegreenalliance.org/news/publications/document/BGA-EPI-Report-vFINAL-MEDIA.pdf

[27] Kelly, G. and Pearce, N. (2010) 'The credibility test', *The Fabian Review*. Available at: http://www.fabians.org.uk/wp-content/uploads/2012/04/FabianReview2010Autumn.pdf

How US politics is undermining the American Dream, and what it means for the UK

Jacob S. Hacker

What does it mean to be middle class? Economic experts talk about levels of income: between two and four times the poverty level, for example, or the middle three quintiles of the income distribution.

When you ask Americans, though, you get a very different answer. First, most Americans believe they *are* middle class; only a small share say they are poor or rich. Second, what defines the middle class for them – according to decades of polling, focus groups and public discourse – is much broader than income: a job with reasonable pay and benefits; the ability to raise a family without undue hardship; basic economic security grounded in the ownership of homes and other assets; and the opportunity to rise up the economic ladder through education and hard work.

All these core aspects of the middle class are under siege in the US and, increasingly, the UK as well. The most unmistakable sign of trouble, as Larry Mishel and Heidi Shierholz show in Chapter 1.1 of this volume, is the stagnation of median wages that has occurred over the last generation as income gains have accrued overwhelmingly to the richest.

But the income squeeze associated with rising inequality is only the most visible tip of a much larger iceberg of middle-class strain. As wages have stagnated, families have gained economic ground mostly by relying on both parents working more – which has created a 'care squeeze' as they juggle paid work and caring for young children or ageing parents. As job-based benefits like health insurance and traditional defined-benefit pensions have eroded or disappeared, middle-class families have borne greater economic risk despite little in the way of greater economic rewards. And the private safety net of savings and wealth on which these families depend has become much more threadbare, especially after the market crisis of 2007.

In short, the ideal and reality of the middle class are increasingly distant. Yet political leaders have been slow to respond to this growing gap and, in crucial areas, have actually made it worse. In this chapter, I examine why, focusing on the US and its lessons for the UK.

The middle class and its discontents

The last generation has witnessed a remarkable turnaround in US economic outcomes. In the generation after the Second World War, the economy and the earnings of all income classes grew roughly in tandem. Since the 1970s, the economy has slowed modestly, but the big change has been where the rewards of growth have gone. In a word, they have gone to the top. Over the last generation, the share of pre-tax national income received by the richest 1% of Americans has more than doubled. The share received by the richest 0.1% has more than *quadrupled*, rising from less than 3% in 1970 to more than 12% in 2007 – the highest proportion since the creation of the income tax in 1913.[1]

This is not a story of stagnant productivity or general economic malaise. It is a story of the decoupling of aggregate productivity and most workers' wages. Even a college-educated entry-level male worker earns barely more than such a worker did a generation ago.[2] While the 1990s economic boom temporarily reduced the pay–productivity gap, the gap returned with a vengeance in the 2000s. Indeed, the 2000s' expansion was the first on record in which a typical family's income was lower at the end than at the close of the prior business cycle.[3]

As job security has eroded and gains have shifted towards the top, other pillars of security and opportunity have also come under strain:

- **Education and social mobility.** Class lines have hardened. US inequality is sky-high; US social mobility is below the advanced industrial norm.[4] The US has gone from the world leader in college completion to a middling performer. More and more of rapidly rising college costs are financed through loans, burdening students and their parents – except for the children of the rich, who gain a huge head start.[5]

- **Pensions and social insurance.** The US's job-based framework of economic security has gone from basic to broken. Defined, secure pensions that promise a guaranteed benefit in retirement – once the hallmark of a good job – are vanishing. Furthermore, 401(k)s and other tax-deferred savings accounts are not filling the gap. As medical costs continue to outstrip inflation, employment-based health insurance benefits are becoming rarer and less protective.[6]

- **Housing and economic assets.** Besides their homes, most middle-class families have strikingly little in the way of private assets to cushion economic shocks or build their futures. And, of course, those homes look far less secure than they once did. The traditional strategy of gradually accumulating wealth through housing has taken a perhaps-fatal hit, with implications for the economic security not just of the middle aged but also of the young aspiring middle class.

- **Balancing work and family.** With families increasingly needing two earners to maintain a middle-class standard of living, their economic calculus has changed in ways that accentuate many of the risks they face. What happens when a parent leaves the workforce to care for children, when a child is chronically ill, when one spouse loses his or her job, or when an elderly parent needs assistance? Precisely because it takes more work and more income to maintain a middle-class standard of living, events that require the care and time of family members produce special strains. This 'care squeeze' creates new risks alongside traditional job concerns.

The political roots of middle-class strains

Who killed the old middle-class social contract? Most explanations focus almost exclusively on the unstoppable forces of technology and globalisation. Computers and automation have reduced the rewards for routine skills and encouraged outsourcing and offshoring. The entry of hundreds of millions of literate low-wage workers into the global workforce has undermined the earning power of middle-class Americans, especially those without a college degree. Compared with these vast tides, the conventional wisdom suggests, US politics and policy have played only a bit role – and can do only a limited amount to reclaim the American Dream.

Technological change and globalisation matter immensely, of course. But their effect in the US (and other nations) has been heavily shaped by whether and how governments have responded to them. After all, these shifts have affected all rich nations – most more so than the US – and yet few have seen anything like the US's sharp upward shift of economic rewards, erosion of economic security or breakdown of social benefits.

Moreover, in many nations where inequality and insecurity have risen, policymakers have pushed back through active labour market policies, taxes and public spending. Not so in the US. Despite the Earned Income Tax Credit for the working poor and expansion of Medicaid health insurance coverage for low-income families and children, low-wage workers have continued to fall behind. According to the Congressional Budget Office, even after all public and private benefits and federal taxes are taken into account, almost 40% of all household income gains between 1979 and 2007 accrued to the richest 1% of Americans – more than received by the bottom 90% combined.[7]

Another clue that politics and policy have been crucial is that the US's newly unequal and insecure economy developed hand in hand with a new politics. As Hacker and Pierson argued in *Winner-take-all politics*,[8] corporate America organised on an unprecedented scale in the late 1970s to influence government policy, not just through campaign-giving, but also with vast lobbying efforts. At the same time, with campaign costs shooting up, money became a far more important resource for politicians – and, as we have seen, a far more unequally distributed resource in US society.

The rising role of money and the increasing imbalance between business and other organised interests fundamentally changed Washington. For the contemporary Republican Party, these changes were welcome and encouraged the party to shift ever rightward on economic issues. Democrats, by contrast, found themselves increasingly torn between their historical commitment to the 'little guy' and the pull of money from the big guys, including, for much of the 1990s and early 2000s, the ascendant titans of Wall Street. The result was an ever more polarised economic debate in which a significant faction of one party, the Democrats, repeatedly proved willing to cut bargains that undermined the middle class's standing.

The recent string of large tax cuts for the richest of Americans have highlighted the long-term role of our tax system in abetting inequality. Far more important and less recognised have been ways in which public policies have remade markets to advantage the top. Failure to enforce federal laws that empower workers to form unions undermined organised labour as a force for good pay and benefits. Corporate governance rules all but asked top executives to drive up their own earnings. Financial deregulation brought great riches for some while pushing many ordinary families into unaffordable loans, and ultimately crashing the economy.

Perhaps the least visible policy changes were passive aggressive in nature – deliberate failures to address changing economic and social conditions, such as the need for families to balance work and family. Entire categories of support that have become essential to middle-class life, such as good childcare, are simply not a public responsibility in the US. Meanwhile, responsibilities that corporations once shouldered are shifting back on to families. Uniquely among industrial nations, the US came to rely on employers as mini-welfare states, providing health insurance, pensions and other benefits that elsewhere enjoyed state sponsorship. But as employers have pulled back, government has not filled the gap, leaving families more vulnerable.

Perhaps it is not surprising, then, that so many middle-class Americans feel abandoned. Asked in mid-2010 whom government had helped 'a great deal' during the downturn: 53% of Americans said banks and financial institutions; 44% fingered large corporations; and just 2% thought economic policies had helped the middle class a great deal.[9]

Lessons for the UK

To what extent has the UK experienced similar trends? In one respect, the parallels are striking. The share of income accruing to the richest in the UK has risen almost as sharply as it has in the US. In 2005, the last year for which data are available for both nations, the proportion of pre-tax income going to the top 1% (excluding capital gains, which cannot be easily compared across the two countries) was 14.25% in the UK, compared with 17.42% in the US.[10]

In the UK, however, this upward shift of income has not occurred alongside stagnation at the middle as it has in the US – at least not until recently. The main explanation appears to be public policy: direct government transfers to the middle and the bottom of the economic ladder. In a careful comparative analysis, the sociologist Lane Kenworthy has found that the income gains of low-income citizens in the last three decades has depended heavily on changes in public taxes and transfers. 'The New Labour governments under Tony Blair and Gordon Brown', he notes, 'increased benefits and/or reduced taxes for low earners, single parents, and pensioners.... [T]hese were big policy shifts, even if not always high-profile ones. They produced a significant rise in the real disposable incomes of poor households.'[11]

In addition, the continued strong role of the National Health Service in providing universal – and comparatively affordable – services stands in stark contrast to the US experience of runaway health costs and declining private coverage. These policy differences may, in turn, reflect the stronger role of labour unions and the greater commitment to the welfare state evidenced by the Labour Party as compared with the Democratic Party. Whatever the cause, the substantial decline in economic security and painfully slow income growth seen in the US does not appear to be the UK story.

Nonetheless, the US experience is looking more and more relevant. In the last decade, the British middle class has begun to experience the same wage and income stagnation that the US middle class has confronted for years. What is more, the economic crisis and subsequent austerity policies have simultaneously increased economic hardship and encouraged a US-style stagnation in policies, as public and employment-based benefits are cut or held steady in the face of rising needs, and initiatives to deal with new risks such as the care needs of an ageing population are pushed off the agenda. For all these reasons, the US experience offers increasingly salient lessons for the UK – three in particular.

Lesson 1: Pay attention to 'predistribution'

When we think of the government's effects on inequality, we think of 'redistribution' – government taxes and transfers that take from some and give to others. And redistribution is certainly a major part of what government does to reduce inequality and insecurity. As noted, the UK has done more to offset the growth in inequality in the market through taxes and transfers than the US has.

Yet there is good reason to look beyond redistribution in thinking about how to tackle inequality and insecurity. In the US, many of the most important changes have been in what might be called 'predistribution' – the way in which the market distributes its rewards in the first place. Policies governing financial markets, the rights of unions and the pay of top executives have all shifted in favour of those at the top, especially the financial and non-financial executives who make up about six in 10 of the richest 0.1% of Americans.[12]

The moral is that reformers need to focus on market reforms that encourage a more equal distribution of economic power and rewards even before government collects taxes or pays out benefits. This is not just because predistribution is crucial. It is also because excessive reliance on redistribution fosters backlash, making taxes more salient and feeding into the conservative critique that the government simply meddles with 'natural' market rewards. And, lastly, it is because societies in which market inequality is high are, ironically, ones where creating common support for government action is often most difficult. Regulation of markets to limit extremes and give the middle class more voice is hardly easy – witness the fight over financial reform in the US. But it is both more popular and more effective than after-the-fact mopping up.

A predistribution agenda should have several elements. First and most obvious, it must involve a commitment to high levels of employment – a necessary but hardly sufficient condition for broadly shared growth. To tackle hyper-concentration of income at the top and protect against financial instability, effective regulation of financial markets and corporate governance are essential – starting with greater transparency and accountability in executive pay-setting. At the high end of the income scale, policies should be designed to encourage countervailing pressures against self-dealing and pay-without-performance from watchdog organisations and shareholder collectives (such as large institutional shareholders). In the middle range, policies should be focused on facilitating the organisation of workers and the creation of opportunities for voice in the workplace, including not just more aggressive protection of those seeking union representation, but also institutional reform, such as 'right to request' laws that give workers protected institutional channels through which to seek better employment arrangements.

Because growing top-heavy inequality creates threats to equality of opportunity as well, special emphasis should be placed on ensuring that small-scale enterprises and start-up entrepreneurs have the access to capital and legal protection necessary to enter into markets and expand. Similarly, ensuring that educational opportunities are broadly distributed – with a special emphasis on early childhood education and adequate support for college completion for less-advantaged students – is also a pressing priority, even if not a panacea for addressing the deep inequality that so threatens basic equality of opportunity today.

Lesson 2: 'Drift' is dangerous

Over the last generation, across a wide range of areas, US public officials have deliberately failed to update policy in the face of changing economic circumstances, allowing outcomes to 'drift' away from a more equal equilibrium.[13] Although particularly pronounced in the US, drift seems characteristic of many rich democracies today as they confront a rapidly changing economy and society and grapple with persistent fiscal constraints. If this is so, preserving existing policies is not the only challenge. The welfare state traditionally understood remains deeply rooted. But the broader environment of the welfare state – a mixed economy characterised by a healthy civil society – is much more vulnerable. It has become abundantly clear that well-functioning markets are not natural or inherently self-correcting; they require continuing public policy updates in a highly dynamic economic world.

To be sure, UK policymakers face nothing like the institutional hurdles that their US counterparts – who are coping with the fragmentation of US governing authority – do. Still, it is worth remembering that many of the most severe causes of drift in the US are extra-constitutional, and thus potentially relevant to UK developments. Partisan polarisation – which in the US at least has involved the conservative pole of the debate moving steadily further to the right – presents inherent barriers to policy updating, reducing the chance of agreement even when there is broad public support for it. Fiscal constraints are another cause of drift, and the tightness of these constraints depends very much on the policy choices of the past. Large shifts in the fiscal constitution of the state, such as major changes in the visibility or source of tax revenues, can powerfully influence the tendency of the political system towards drift.

To protect and restore a well-functioning market democracy, therefore, those worried about inequality and insecurity must preserve an effective capacity for robust governance. They should resist institutional reforms that abet gridlock and ensure that policies put in place retain the capacity for over-time adjustment, whether automatically (as in benefits indexed to wages or prices) or structurally (through the preservation of basic regulatory, tax and spending powers that are too often sacrificed on the conservative altar of privatisation and delegation).

Lesson 3: Increase the organisational might of the middle

As documented at length in *Winner-take-all politics*,[14] the transformation of the US's political economy over the last generation has far less to do with the shifting demands of voters than with the changing organisational balance between concentrated economic interests and the broad public. Indeed, the sharp shift of policy towards the affluent and business occurred despite remarkable stability in public views on many economic issues – including views on government redistribution, progressive tax policy and the importance of key programmes of economic security. The agenda disconnect that we see today, as politicians ignore Americans' concerns about the lack of jobs in favour of cutting programmes that the public likes and preserving tax reductions for the rich that it does not, is not new. It has characterised the politics of the last generation.

The root of the problem, once again, is organisational. As Theda Skocpol has argued, middle-class democracy rested on organisations, such as unions and cross-class civic organisations, that gave middle-class voters knowledge about what was at stake in policy debates and political leverage to influence these debates.[15] Without this organisational grounding, voters simply have a very hard time drawing connections between what politicians do and the strains they face in their lives, much less formulating a broad idea of how those strains could be effectively addressed.

A revival of middle-class organisations will necessarily require moving beyond the traditional base of such movements, namely, organised labour and old-line fraternal organisations, to encompass new social movements and the harnessing of new technologies. Where such initiative will come from is inherently difficult to foresee, but three trends give at least some cause for optimism. The first is that the start-up costs of organisational development have dramatically fallen over the last generation. The second is the widespread dissatisfaction with existing policy and political alignments seen in the US and other wealthy nations. The third – and most up for grabs – is the typical pattern of new leaders emerging out of crisis moments to galvanise citizens around shared concerns.

Ironically, since the economic crisis, these trends have mostly benefited conservative movements. In the US, the most effective organising has taken place not on the left, but on the right, with the rise of the loose organisation of conservative voters, right-wing media figures and corporate-funded ideological activists that travels under the 'Tea Party' banner. But there is good reason to believe that many of the forces that impelled these developments also have the potential to galvanise progressive movements in the coming years, especially as the Tea Party agenda moves from gauzy ideals to concrete (and deeply unpopular) policies.

Indeed, the Tea Party's success should be instructive for all organisational reformers. It rests on the combination of champions inside government and organisers working at the grassroots. It has a clear agenda (scale back government) and enemy (President Obama). And it has effectively utilised both old-style organising through local chapters and new communications technologies (and, yes, has also benefited from lavish financing from deep-pocketed donors, including many from corporate quarters). While the Tea Party cannot and should not be simply emulated by those seeking to reconstruct middle-class democracy, its three key features – grassroots organising linked to national reform leaders, a forward-looking vision that is directed against a perceived contemporary threat and the use of flexible participatory modes enabled by new media – are contemporary preconditions for effective organising.

This diagnosis is both encouraging and challenging. It is encouraging because there is nothing natural about the harsh divisions that have arisen in the US. They are rooted in politics and policy, not the inexorable forces of globalisation or technological change. In many cases, moreover, they require not major programmes of redistribution – never easy to enact – but measures to reshape the market so that it distributes its rewards more broadly in the first place.

The challenge, however, is that reforms to tackle middle-class strains will require using a broken political system to fix a broken political system: the main obstacle to change and the main vehicle for change are one and the same. This catch-22 affords no easy resolution. But it does suggest where reformers' energies should be directed, and it points to opportunities that are too often missed by those narrowly focused on rhetorical messages and strategic moves.

Perhaps the most important implication is that those seeking to achieve a new governing economic philosophy will have to rebuild the organisational foundations of democratic capitalism. An inspiring economic vision will be grounded in an institutional blueprint for using active democratic government to meet the challenges facing US society – challenges that are increasingly facing the US's great ally across the Atlantic.

Notes

[1] Hacker, J. and Pierson, P. (2011) *Winner-take-all politics: how Washington made the rich richer – and turned its back on the middle class*, New York, NY: Simon & Schuster, ch 1.

[2] Ibid, p 36.

[3] Greenstein, R., Parrott, S. and Sherman, A. (2008) 'Poverty and share of Americans without health insurance were higher in 2007—and median income for working age households was lower', Washington, DC: Center on Budget and Policy Priorities. Available at: www.cbpp.org/cms/?fa=view&id=621

[4] Organisation for Economic Co-operation and Development (OECD) (2010) *A family affair: intergenerational social mobility across OECD countries*, Paris: OECD. Available at: www.oecd.org/dataoecd/2/7/45002641.pdf

[5] College Board Advocacy and Policy Center (2010) 'Trends in student aid'. Available at: http://trends.collegeboard.org/downloads/archives/SA_2010.pdf

[6] Hacker, J. and Pierson, P. (2008) *The great risk shift: the new economic insecurity and the decline of the American Dream*, New York, NY: Oxford University Press.

[7] Congressional Budget Office (2010) 'Average federal taxes by income group'. Available at: http://www.cbo.gov/publication/42870

[8] Hacker and Pierson (2011), op cit.

[9] Pew Research Center (2010) 'Government economic policies seen as boon for banks and big business, not middle class or poor'. Available at: http://pewresearch.org/pubs/1670/large-majorities-say-govt-stimulus-policies-mostly-helped-banks-financial-institutins-not-middle-class-or-poor

[10] Paris School of Economics (2011) 'Top incomes: a global perspective'. Available at: http://g-mond.parisschoolofeconomics.eu/topincomes/

[11] Kenworthy, L. (2010) 'Has rising inequality been bad for the poor?'. Available at: http://lanekenworthy.net/2010/12/14/has-rising-inequality-been-bad-for-the-poor/. Also, Kenworthy, L. (2010) 'Has the rise in income inequality been Rawlsian?'. Available at: www.u.arizona.edu/~lkenwor/hastheriseinincomeinequalitybeenrawlsian.pdf

[12] Hacker and Pierson (2011), op cit, p 46.

[13] Hacker, J. (2004) 'Privatizing risk without privatizing the welfare state', *American Political Science Review*, vol 98, no 2, pp. 243-60.

[14] Hacker and Pierson (2011), op cit.

[15] Skocpol, T. (2004) *Diminished democracy: from membership to management in American civic life*, Norman, OK: University of Oklahoma.

Conclusion: learning the lessons

Vidhya Alakeson

The UK has been navigating unchartered waters in recent years. The fall in living standards experienced by families on low to middle incomes has been unparalleled in the post-war era. According to the Institute for Fiscal Studies, families on median incomes have experienced an unprecedented collapse in living standards.[1] The coming years do not present much change in fortunes. Forecasts suggest that, even if robust growth returns after 2017, incomes for the low- to middle-income group in the UK will be no higher in 2020 than they were in 2007.[2] With growth assumptions having to be revised downwards on a regular basis and the future of the eurozone still very uncertain, even this level of improvement may be optimistic.

It is clear that the trends facing low- to middle-income families in the UK have been longer lasting in the US. While ordinary workers did benefit from certain periods of growth in the US, notably, in the mid- to late 1990s, as Lane Kenworthy highlights in Chapter 1.2, overall their earnings have been flat since the late 1970s.

If the forecasts are gloomy, the impact of falling living standards on British people's lives has been difficult for some. For those on middle incomes, this new economic landscape has come as a surprise. Aspirations such as home-ownership that were expected by their parents are increasingly the preserve of the better off. Forecasts indicate that if the economic recovery is weak, 27% of low- to middle-income families with children could be renting privately in England by 2025 and as many as 35% in London, with mortgaged home-ownership falling significantly.[3] Reasonable rewards, like the ability to go on short holidays, now seem a struggle. Meanwhile, for many on lower incomes, day-to-day life has become a struggle. Increases in the cost of living continue to outpace wages, families are feeling the weight of debt repayments and austerity has led to major cuts in government support for tax credits and services. Among those hardest hit, families are turning to food banks, pawn shops and subprime lending to get by – features of life more traditionally associated with poverty and being out of work.

Added to these immediate problems is a store of future problems that will shape the lives of the next generation. Most urgent among these is youth unemployment. More than a million young people are currently unemployed and the evidence is clear that long periods of early unemployment affect job prospects over the long term.[4] The decision to scrap the Education Maintenance Allowance that encouraged young people from less well-off backgrounds to stay in education will also have negative effects on future prospects. While the government may be holding itself to account for the improvement it can make to social mobility, today's economic reality will undermine some of its ambition.

This collection of chapters from leading US experts acts both as a warning and a source of reassurance for the UK. Given the similarities between our two labour markets, the US sends us a warning that we should heed. However, the authors are also clear that the US situation is not the inevitable outcome of global and technological trends. Economic and social policy choices, and the loss of power by the middle class in political decision-making, have amplified these trends when they could have made them better. On a more positive note, the US is also an engine of innovation in many areas, as Keith Wardrip discusses in Chapter 2.5 in relation to affordable housing. Its federal structure allows for far more experimentation than the UK's more centralised state, offering the UK possible solutions as well as warnings.

In many respects, the UK has a head start over the US in shaping a better future for those on low to middle incomes: it has a stronger welfare state, stronger employment protections and people accept a larger role for government action in addressing economic challenges than in the US. As such, we can also offer lessons and solutions to those on the other side of the Atlantic. Recent policy decisions may be taking the UK towards, rather than away from, a US-style future: cuts to tax credits and childcare support coupled with a tax cut for the wealthiest will not serve those on low to middle incomes well. But the collection of chapters highlights four important areas for policy action if we are to avoid some of the choices that have been made in the US and build a more balanced recovery and a better future for those on low to middle incomes.

Achieving better wage growth

The first and perhaps the most difficult of the four areas is the need to focus on what workers achieve in the market through employment and wages, not just the outcomes of government redistribution, what Jacob Hacker in Chapter 3.2 calls 'predistribution'. Workers in the bottom half of earnings have been taking home a smaller share of the UK's wage pot since the 1970s, even when the economy was growing strongly.[5] In the 2000s, this meant that tax credits had to do more to prop up family incomes. But efforts to rein in public spending are now limiting investment in tax credits. In Chapter 2.4, Daniel Gitterman highlights the limitations of tax credits, arguing that in straitened economic circumstances, governments on both sides of the Atlantic will need to focus on boosting pay packets to cut the tax credit bill for the public purse.

One of the challenges of improving market outcomes for workers in the US and the UK is the scale of the low-wage labour market. As Mayhew and Holmes highlight, the growth of low-wage jobs is in part the result of skills-biased technological change but, more importantly, the result of the demise of union membership and the reach of collective bargaining on both sides of the Atlantic.[6] Just over 20% of workers in the UK are in low-wage jobs, according to the OCED's definition of low-wage work, and, as Applebaum and Leana discuss in Chapter 2.1, low-wage sectors such as care are set to expand. While the National Minimum Wage has removed the excesses of poor wages in the UK without negative effects on employment, it falls far behind the wage level necessary for a basic standard of living. The value of the federal minimum wage in the US has been allowed to fall over time and the UK minimum wage has also failed to keep pace with inflation since the mid-2000s.[7] Upwards pressure on the minimum wage in both countries will be important in maintaining an acceptable wage floor.

Campaigns such as the Living Wage have successfully improved the wages of workers on both sides of the Atlantic but, by the very nature of a voluntary mechanism, progress has been patchy. In the US context, Living Wage campaigns have improved wages in the public sector by ensuring that those employed through outsourced contracts are paid a living wage. Local authorities in the UK are moving in a similar direction and could learn from their US counterparts. In the private sector, progress has been largely confined to sectors in the UK such as finance, where low-wage workers are in the minority. Recent analysis shows that large companies in certain sectors could afford to go further. Implementing the UK Living Wage would add less than 1% to the wage bill of large firms in construction, banking and food production, without taking into consideration any other adjustments that could further reduce costs such as improvements in productivity.[8] This suggests that campaigners and the government should keep up pressure on these companies to increase their pay.

Beyond these voluntary measures, policymakers need to shine a light on those businesses who do better by their workers. More transparency not just on executive pay, but also on pay at the bottom, will help to raise the issue in the public consciousness. Few companies want a reputation as a minimum-wage employer, so greater transparency around pay at the bottom end of the scale could helpfully put upwards pressure on wages. In addition, the government needs to proactively work with industry to focus on improving skills and productivity within low-paid sectors as a route to better pay for workers. There are interesting examples to build on, for example, the American retailer Costco. Costco pays above-average wages to attract the best employees and offers career progression to retain them.[9] This is in contrast to other major US retailers who tend to pay poorly, offer little chance of progression and have higher turnover. The government could offer businesses support and financial incentives to choose the high-productivity, high-wage road rather than a low-productivity, low-wage business model.

Meaningful protection against risks

The second important policy area is to develop new forms of economic security and protection for workers. In the past, union membership, permanent employment contracts and workplace organisation guaranteed workers a certain level of security, even if wages were low. As Lane Kenworthy notes in Chapter 1.2, international evidence unequivocally highlights the importance of unions and collective bargaining agreements in improving conditions for workers. However, he is rightly pessimistic that the decline of unions will be reversed in the US, and the same scepticism applies to the UK.

Work for many people is now characterised by insecurity and fragmentation, with little ability to organise for better terms and conditions or higher pay, or even to know what a fair deal for the work in question is. Even for those in a permanent job, the threat of redundancy and unemployment is currently very real. The sharp end of this situation is well illustrated by Carré and Heintz in their discussion of temporary workers in the US (Chapter 2.2) and by Appelbaum and Leana in the context of care workers (Chapter 2.1). In the UK, public service reform is creating new challenges for workers in its drive to improve choice and control for people who use services, for example, through the introduction of personal budgets in social care or removing schools from local authority control through free schools. There is a role for policy in developing and supporting new forms of protection for workers that respond to today's insecurities. This could include new roles for unions but could also include other social actors.

Part of this debate in the UK has focused on reshaping the role of the welfare state away from a large number of small benefits to focus on protecting people against the major economic risks of life:

unemployment, having a child, serious illness and old age.[10] More tangible protections around these important areas could reinvigorate people's commitment to a tax-funded welfare state as well as providing a greater sense of security in a fluid labour market. Unemployment insurance has been proposed as one way of protecting those who have worked, but may have a spell of unemployment, from a serious decline in living standards and the need to rely on government benefits.[11] Others have suggested restoring the guarantee of a job for young people who have been unemployed for more than six months, as this would provide protection against the long-term scarring of youth unemployment.[12]

Another angle on protection is the need to develop intermediaries that can support atomised workers to organise for better terms and conditions and provide group access to benefits such as pensions and training. In Chapter 2.1, Appelbaum and Leana highlighted the positive role that intermediaries in some US states have played in helping to organise care workers, underpinned by supportive legislation. In the British context, there is renewed interest in mutuals and employee-owned enterprises as one route to improving outcomes for workers, particularly as the public sector divests itself of much of its own provision.

Savings and assets are another central pillar to the development of economic security and protection. As Smith-Ramani and Mehta highlight in Chapter 2.6, assets provide a safety net as well as a springboard to opportunity. Both the UK and the US have poor records on savings by international standards. The savings ratio in the UK was at a 30-year low in 2008 according to the Office for National Statistics. Among the low- to middle-income group, 67% have less than one month's savings to fall back on, although experts advise having at least three months' income in savings.[13] This is all the more significant given the incredibly high barriers to home-ownership that low- to middle-income families now face, as Keith Wardrip discusses in Chapter 2.5. This makes it harder for them to accumulate wealth through housing and places greater emphasis on other forms of asset-building. ✓

The government's decision to scrap matched savings programmes such as the Child Trust Fund and the Savings Gateway is a step backwards in ensuring adequate protection for families given the importance of matching in creating incentives for low-income people to save. Access to affordable credit is a related and important dimension of this type of protection. For many people in the low- to middle-income group, credit was freely available in the run-up to the crisis. This has led to large amounts of debt but also to an inability to access mainstream credit and a push into the subprime market, where interest rates are cripplingly high. Access to more affordable, better-regulated credit through credit unions and other non-profit organisations will support families to weather storms and reach aspirations for which savings alone are not adequate.

The new needs of working families

While balancing work and family commitments has long been difficult for working parents, the growth of atypical working hours coupled with the growth of dual-earning households poses a more serious challenge to the reconciliation of work and parenthood. This is the third important area for policy development raised by this volume. Addressing these pressures will have a material impact on living standards going forward by keeping women, in particular, in work and contributing to family income. All too often, caring responsibilities force women out of the labour market against their will. Women's employment has become increasingly important for low- to middle-income households in the UK, filling the gap left by declining employment among men. In 1968, 71% of net household income in the low- to middle-income group came from male employment and 11% from women's employment. By 2008/09, only 40% came from men's work and 24% from women's.[14]

Balancing work and family life is particularly challenging for low- to middle-income families for several reasons. First, they are under greater financial pressure then higher-income parents and are more likely to need to have both parents in work to maintain their living standards. Second, they are more likely to work in sectors in the UK that require atypical hours of work such as retail, health and social care, and hotels and restaurants. Third, they cannot always afford to buy the services that would help relieve some of the pressures they face, for example, adequate, flexible childcare or care for ageing family members. At the same time, they are often too well off to receive much support from government towards these costs. Finally, individuals in low- to middle-income households are less likely to enjoy the kinds of autonomy and flexibility at work that can help them juggle work and family.[15]

These pressures put renewed emphasis on investment in childcare and eldercare. The UK government has recognised childcare as an important new frontier of the welfare state rather than the private concern of families and has invested significantly in services for under fives, making it a role model for the US according to several authors. However, parents continue to report difficulties finding childcare they can afford. The UK continues to have some of the most expensive childcare in the world. Financial support for childcare has also been cut in the last two years, leaving families facing difficult choices about whether or not it pays to have a second person in work. On care for older people, the UK has a much poorer record. Despite numerous reviews, decisions about the best way to fund social care have been put off time and again, including by the current government. This leaves in place a means-tested social care system that is increasingly poorly funded and only able to provide for those with the highest levels of need, much like the Medicaid long-term care system in the US. The vast majority of people are unprepared for the future costs of care, with catastrophic consequences for those who may end up living with dementia or a similarly disabling condition. Family members are filling in the gaps left by the failure of policy in this area, with women in their 50s often being forced to leave the labour market to care for elderly relatives.

Alongside the need for investment in services that support families to fulfil their caring responsibilities, there is also a need for greater employer flexibility. This can reduce the need for expensive childcare, keep parents in work and improve the quality of family life. In a recent survey about the price of motherhood, around a third of mothers of young children on low to middle incomes said that they would prefer to work longer hours but the high costs of childcare and the lack of workplace flexibility forced them to work part time.[16] Respondents wanted better access to term-time-only working, compressed hours and the ability to work more frequently from home, all of which could support them to work longer hours and still manage their family commitments. The government is proposing to extend the right to request flexible working to all employees, not just those with caring responsibilities. While this is likely to help families by making flexible working mainstream and not the preserve of working mothers, there is more that needs to be done to make flexibility a reality for those who already benefit from a legal right. Public sector organisations can take the lead and the government can act as a greater champion of those private sector employers that have shown leadership in this area.

Voice, power and decision-making

The fourth important area for policy development that emerges from this volume is to ensure that those who are less well off in the UK can find a collective voice and represent their views in public debate. It is hard to see how broad-based prosperity can be achieved unless those who have most to gain from achieving better growth are active participants in decision-making processes. Previous forms of participation, notably, membership of unions and political parties, have lost power and significance and, therefore, new organisations and structures are required.

In the workplace context, there is growing interest in formal structures to give workers a greater say, such as worker representation on remuneration committees and company boards and employee engagement in decisions about how firms invest in training and development.[17] However, there are also grassroots approaches to organising that are gathering momentum on both sides of the Atlantic and aim to empower workers to push for a fairer deal themselves outside of any formal structures. The Living Wage campaign described earlier is perhaps the best example. It was started in the UK by parents in London who felt that working two minimum-wage jobs left no time for family life and did not bring in enough money to allow the family to meet an acceptable living standard. As Jacob Hacker suggests in Chapter 3.2, there is much that can be learned from the organising strategies of the Tea Party movement and its use of technology, which can be put to more positive, progressive ends.

In the broader social context, there are many routes for low- to middle-income families to shape opportunities for themselves and their children, for example, by working as childminders, setting up free schools, standing as independent police commissioners and local councillors, and developing other local services. There is a tendency to think of the group being on the receiving end of the negative consequences of the economy. But they can be important economic actors and authors of their own outcomes.

A squeezed decade

The coming years will not be easy for ordinary workers in the UK. Wages are unlikely to reach their pre-recession level for many years to come. But the US experience cautions against a myopic focus on GDP growth. Focusing on GDP growth alone carries the risk that the UK will also experience a lost generation that faces a breakdown in the societal promise that if you do your part and work hard, you can expect to achieve a decent standard of living in return. It is true that the balance of opinion among economists in the UK is already starting to shift away from a single-minded focus on deficit reduction now that the economy has entered a double-dip recession. In fact, advocacy for greater public sector investment from President Obama has helped bolster the case for a rethink on the big macroeconomic judgements of our day. But, as yet, the government has done little to argue for a broader-based recovery which ensures that growth, when it does come, is shared with all. As Tamara Draut rightly points out in Chapter 3.1, that will require more than just a return to economic growth. It will require a focus on investment and policy action in the four areas described earlier to ensure that the future fruits of growth are more evenly shared and we rebuild not only the strength of the UK economy but also the living standards of ordinary working families.

Notes

[1] Brewer, M., Browne, J. and Joyce, R. (2011) *Child and working age poverty from 2010–2020*, London: Institute for Fiscal Studies.

[2] Whittaker, M. (2010) *The essential guide to squeezed Britain: the annual audit of low to middle income households*, London: Resolution Foundation.

[3] Whitehead, C., Williams, P., Tang, C. and Udagawa, C. (2012) *Housing in transition: understanding the dynamics of tenure change*, London: Resolution Foundation and Shelter Housing.

[4] Gregg, P. and Tominey, E. (2004) 'The wage scar from youth unemployment', CMPO Working Paper Series No 04/097, University of Bristol.

[5] Whittaker, M. and Savage, L. (2011) *Missing out: why ordinary workers are experiencing growth without gain*, London: Resolution Foundation.

[6] Holmes, C. and Mayhew, K. (2012) *The changing shape of the UK job market and its implications for the bottom half of earners*, London: Resolution Foundation.

[7] Manning A. (2012) *Minimum wage: maximum impact*, London: Resolution Foundation.

[8] Pennycook, M. (2012) *What price a living wage: understanding the impact of a living wage on firm-level wage bills*, London: Resolution Foundation and Institute for Public Policy Research.

[9] Ton, Z. (2010) 'Why good jobs are good for retailers', *Harvard Business Review*. Available at: http://hbr.org/2012/01/why-good-jobs-are-good-for-retailers

[10] Purnell, J. (2012) 'We need a welfare state that secures Beveridge's legacy', *Financial Times*, 2 March.

[11] Cooke, G. (2011) *National salary insurance: reforming the welfare state to provide real protection*, London: Institute for Public Policy Research.

[12] Timms, S. (2012) *Job guarantee: a right and responsibility to work*, London: The Smith Institute.

[13] Whittaker, M. (2012) *The essential guide to squeezed Britain: the annual audit of low to middle income households*, London: Resolution Foundation.

[14] Brewer, M. and Wren-Lewis, L. (2011) 'Why did Britain's households get richer? Decomposing UK household income growth between 1968 and 2008–09', Institute for Fiscal Studies analysis for the Resolution Foundation Commission on Living Standards.

[15] Alakeson, V. (2011) *Childcare: failing to meet the needs of working parents*, London: Resolution Foundation.

[16] Alakeson, V. (2012) *The price of motherhood: women and part-time work*, London: Resolution Foundation.

[17] High Pay Commission (2011) 'Cheques with balances: why tackling high pay is in the national interest'. Available at: http://highpaycommission.co.uk/wp-content/uploads/2011/11/HPC_final_report_WEB.pdf

Index

Page references for notes are followed by n